Devon Trolly Lace

The lost lace of the
East Devon Coast

Carol McFadzean

First published 2004 by
Carol McFadzean,   Barn Cottage, Broadway, Woodbury,
                          Devon. EX5 1NY

©Carol McFadzean 2004

ISBN   0-9547683-0-2

Typesetting by the author, pattern graphics by Short Run Press.
Printed by Short Run Press, Exeter, Devon.

Contents

Forward

This incredible collection of over seven hundred samples of Devon Trolly Lace has been one of the most important lace finds of recent years. I remember being so excited when I handled this buried treasure for the first time shortly after it had been unearthed in Woodbury Salterton Primary School.

Since then it has been a voyage of discovery for those involved in following new trails in the quest for information about the lace and the original lace makers. The recreation of the patterns and samples of lace has been a labour of love for all those who have worked with Carol McFadzean on the project. One feels it must have been very different for the Woodbury Salterton workers who were striving to feed themselves and their families. I would like to think of this book as a memorial to them and their skills.

This is only the beginning of the search for a better understanding of this 'lost lace' and I feel privileged to have been part of the quest.

Patricia J. Bury
2004

Acknowledgements

I am indebted to the governors of Woodbury Salterton C of E Primary School, particularly the Chair of Governors, Susan Jones and Andrea Brown, Headteacher, for allowing me to research and take 'temporary ownership' of the lace find. To Gill Selley, the 'finder' of the lace I owe so much, as her enthusiasm for local history is infectious and knows no limit.

I would like to acknowledge the assistance given to me by the staff of all the Museums that I visited, in particular Alexandra McCulloch of Aylesbury Museum, Marion Nicholls of Luton Museum, Sarah Orton of Northampton Museum and Pat Perryman and Margaret Lewis from Allhallows Museum, Honiton. Special thanks must go to Shelly Tobin, Curator of Textiles at the Royal Albert Memorial Museum, Exeter, whose interest in the lace find was very encouraging and who ably assisted my research into the 'lost lace' by providing unlimited access to the relevant materials at the museum. I am also thankful for the assistance of the staff at the Devon Record Office and the West Country Studies Library in Exeter and to Rosemary Green, Librarian at 'The Hollies', the headquarters of The Lace Guild in the U.K. My gratitude has to be expressed to the lace makers who assisted me in my research: the OIDFA members who forwarded snippets of information from afar, Pamela Nottingham, who gave her advice and assistance so freely, Joan Blanchard and Shelley Canning for their knowledge of Malmesbury lace and Downton lace respectively.

For assistance with the illustrations I am indebted to Shirley Pavey, Sally Reason, Maureen Parnell and Alison Parker for the loan of Trolly bobbins and machine lace and to Roger Stokes for images from the Woodbury Photographic Archive. Permission to produce the negative of Amelia Dixon was given by Bonhams Auctioneers, The Knowle, and the portrait owner Enrico Paoletti in Italy. I am grateful to Geoff Downs, of 'Itsa Bobbins' for making the set of Trolly bobbins with which I experimented and to 'Mainly Lace' and 'Roseground Supplies' for producing a bean bag pillow and thread for further experimentation.

Finally I owe my husband Ian special thanks for his assistance with the reprographics and my computer problems! His continued support and humour when times were hard made this mammoth task much easier.

I must express my never ending gratitude to those lace colleagues who have spent many hours trialling and making some of the lace samples for this publication. To Christine Akhurst, Ada Archer, Kate Arnfield, Caroline Biggins, Edna Brown, Pauline Cochrane, Mary Gibbons, Ellie Govier, Pat Hansford, Milada Marshall, Beryl Maw, Sue Morgan, Mary de Salis, Alison Thoburn, and Liz Trebble many many thanks. In the struggle to make the lace and solve the mysteries of the samples the lace makers have been most ably assisted by Trish Bury, who became the 'unofficial' lace consultant and tutor for the find and who also got 'caught up' in the search for new information. For her advice, support and encouragement we all thank her.

OLD LACE

Yellowed with years and musty,
A bit of rare old lace –
Nobody knew it's history,
Nor had found it's hiding place

'Til deep in the darkest corner,
Of an old and airy loft,
Wrapped in a dealer's linen bag,
It had secretly taken rest.

Amongst the rafters and roof tiles,
And other items of old,
These tiny scraps of ancient lace,
Had a story to unfold.

Someone, now a memory,
Had silently laid it there,
With dreams and reminiscences,
With heartache and with prayer.

That someone folded it up long ago,
And with tears had tucked it away,
Until we opened that dealer's bag,
It had lain as they wished it to stay.

Some people laugh at the memories,
That cling though the centuries roll,
But some there are who yet believe,
That old lace has a soul!.

Adapted from a poem published in
the I.O.L. November 1977.

A WONDERFUL WEEK IN WOODBURY!

This article first appeared in 'Lace' October 2002 –The Lace Guild magazine

I have always believed in coincidence as a concept and one week in early May was a wonderful example.

I am the archivist for the Local History Group in my village and we were holding an exhibition '50 years in Woodbury Parish' to celebrate the Queen's Golden Jubilee. Gill Selley, the group's Secretary and I were sorting through the archives to see what was useful for the exhibition and whilst doing so she told me of a newspaper cutting that she had recently found that might be of interest to me. Over a cup of coffee, I was shown the cutting, which was from The Times Newspaper, January 9th 1841, and reported that:
"Her Majesty the Queen has graciously commanded a further order of lace from the destitute lace makers of Woodbury Salterton in Devon. Her Majesty has also condescended to receive from them a lace frock for the Princess Royal and has in return sent a munificent present to the lace-makers".
This was naturally of great interest to me as a lace maker and as I had already undertaken considerable research into the subject of lace making in Woodbury Parish it was another piece of the jigsaw to slot in. I went home a 'happy girl' at the end of that Tuesday morning.

Imagine how I felt on the following Monday evening when I returned home from a meeting to find that Gill had called and left a package for me to 'see if it was anything interesting'; the package had been found by Gill in Woodbury Salterton Primary School, whilst looking for more exhibition material. I settled down in the chair and opened a very crumpled linen bag bound with red serge tape. The first thing I removed was a pale green satin handkerchief, that had an unusual edging of white and tarnished silver lace, two Honiton motifs, one being a Crown with Rose, Thistle and Shamrock and some Honiton Rib writing that said "To her most Gracious Majesty, Queen Victoria, with humble gratitude from the poor lace makers of Woodbury Salterton". My hands shook, I went cold and very very quiet, in fact so quiet that my husband asked of I was all right – I am not noted for my silence!! The second piece removed from the bag was also on pale green satin and was a Sampler for the Queen, which stated in Honiton rib "To her most Gracious Majesty with the humble hope of future orders" and below it were samples of lace that looked at first glance like Bucks Point edgings. The widths varied from 1-10cms in depth. My initial thought was 'Why Bucks Point in Devon?', then my history of lace kicked in and I thought 'Devon Trolly', is this what is on my lap?. The third article removed was a small sachet in the same pale green satin, perhaps for the handkerchief, and this had an edging that was slightly Torchon in appearance but again contained the silver thread, now tarnished.

The remaining contents of the bag were old pieces of paper, parchment and fabric that contained numerous samples of what I was now beginning to believe was Devon Trolly lace. I roughly estimated there to be well over 200 samples. As you can well imagine I was getting extremely excited by this time and my brain and vocal cords were in overdrive about what this was, what we had to do next, how we found out about it etc. etc.. Finally there was a letter in the bag from Budleigh Salterton Museum, not dated, but from the text pre 1970, where the contents of the bag had been shown to Mrs Whittaker, a Honiton lace teacher who had confirmed that the samples were in fact Devon Trolly Lace. The bag and contents had been returned to the Headteacher of the school and it had been put away in a box for 'safe keeping'.

When Gill returned to see me the next day and I told her the full story, there were then two very excited 'ladies' in my lounge, both excited because of the local history aspect of the find and one (me) over the moon at having such an historical lace find to handle. We both attended a meeting of the School Governors to inform them of what they 'owned' and they granted permission for Gill and myself to research the find, agreed to a personal request from me to put the find on show publicly for the first time at the OIDFA Congress in Nottingham - the theme was 'The Social History of British Laces' – what could be more 'social' than this find and they are currently thinking that it will be placed on permanent loan to a local museum for future study by lace makers. If you attended the OIDFA Congress I hope you enjoyed seeing this historical coup.

As I write this article the OIDFA Congress is only a week away and if I was wondering what I was going to do with my time when my role as Congress Secretary ended, I have the answer in my hands. The task of researching this find has already begun but will now begin in earnest. My estimate of 200 samples was way out, we, (that is the ever helpful husband), have scanned over 700 samples into the computer for reference, that will need to be studied, redrawn and worked – that should keep me busy!!! We have found initials to look up, have identified one lace maker from 1841 whose name is on the back of one sheet of samples and also identified where she lived in Woodbury Salterton; the initials on the outside of the bag are leading us to a shopkeeper in Woodbury, who if identified as the original owner of the bag lived in the cottage next door to me – as you can imagine, each discovery brings new excitement and further leads.

As a final note I believe I have been incredibly lucky to have experienced the emotions I felt when opening that bag; it was an evening that I shall never forget. I also feel privileged in being permitted to handle and research such a find; my enthusiasm knows no limits and I can't wait to really get going post OIDFA. However having studied all the old books that I, my lace colleagues, and the Devon Record Office and West Country Study Library possess I have a reasonable amount on Devon Trolly Lace, BUT, if any other lace makers have any information that would be helpful in researching this major lace find Gill and I would be very pleased to hear from you. A publication on this terrific discovery will be forthcoming at some point – so watch this space.

Woodbury Salterton Primary School

Woodbury Salterton Village Centre – 1908
Courtesy of Woodbury Photographic Archive

1   *The Woodbury Salterton Lace Find*

Since that article was published, the Woodbury Salterton Lace Find has become an integral part of my life and this publication is the result of my research into this lost lace.

That lace making has been an industry in Devonshire is well documented in specialist history books, therefore I shall not attempt to expand on the subject. In identifying the majority of the content of the bag to be Devon Trolly Lace I set about researching this mainly unknown type of Devonshire lace – what a task!. Very little had been written about it as informational lace books rather than pattern books, as we know them today, were not available until Mrs Bury Palliser first published 'The History of Lace', in 1865. In studying a vast array of historical lace books it has been extremely difficult to verify statements made by eminent lace persons; in fact, identifying the original source of any information was taxing as many of the sections explaining Devon Trolly Lace were identical in wording – so the origin of the facts was impossible to conclude. In endeavouring to answer the questions I posed myself, I have included quotes from many books and have taken them to be substantiated unless I could prove otherwise.

I wanted to discover the answers to the most obvious questions about the lace content of the bag:

What types of lace were contained on the paper and fabric sample pages and how many different patterns were in the bag?

What exactly was Devon Trolly Lace?

When was Trolly Lace introduced into Devonshire and by whom?

Who made it, with what, during what period and in what area of East Devon?

What did it cost for the consumers – what would it cost at today's prices?

What items of clothing did it decorate and how else was it used?

Were the Trolly Lace patterns different from, similar to or the same as the Trolly laces of Buckinghamshire, Bedfordshire, Northamptonshire, Suffolk and Yorkshire?

How did the laces of nearby Downton and Malmesbury relate to those of Devon and was there a connection?

So many questions and each answer producing more – but that was the task in hand; continuing research would be the answer and would probably never be concluded. The final task, and perhaps the most exhilarating for any lace maker, was to redraw and rework the original patterns contained within the bag. My fingers itched to get going, but a logical and sequential approach was required for the mammoth task ahead of me.

In addition to the numerous Devon Trolly Lace samples, the linen bag contained

⊗   a few Torchon edgings and insertions,

⊗   a few Honiton lace edgings mounted on to machine net,

⊗   some wide edgings that resembled early Flemish lace,

⊗   samples of varying widths made from heavier linen thread ,

⊗   a 3 inch wide piece of pulled thread work embroidery, still attached to the waxed linen.

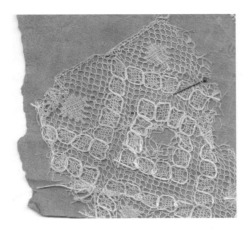 

Torchon designs

Honiton lace edgings

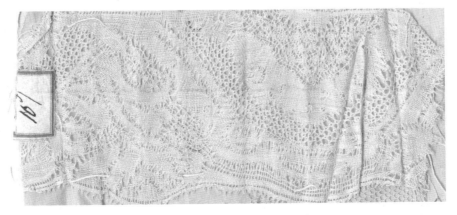

Flemish lace design

Early Flemish design

Pulled threadwork

The bag also contained a letter from 'Fairlynch', the Budleigh Salterton Arts Centre and Museum to Mr Dearnley, the then Headteacher of the school. It was as follows:

Dear Mr Durnley,

I enclose a receipt for the parcel of lace that you lent to me, with apologies for the delay.

I showed the lace to Mrs Whittaker who as you probably know, is one of the chief makers of Honiton lace.

She was most interested. Apparently the lettering on the cushion cover etc. is Honiton lace & the samples are Devon Trolly – but she does not think it could have been made by children as it says on the paper cover.

We hope to have a good section of Honiton lace made locally in the nineteenth century, for our Summer season 1970. Any information or names of anyone who might have made this lace would be very welcome. And if by chance there is any lace bobbins available on loan – this would be invaluable.

As it is our Mayflower'70 next year we are planning our main exhibition with emigration to America in the seventeenth century in mind.

Any information on local emigrants would also be very welcome.

Yours Sincerely

Joy Gowne

I think that this letter shows how dismissive of Trolly Lace people have been in the past as there are only three lines of the letter devoted to it before returning to the subject of Honiton lace. The 'paper cover' mentioned in the letter was not in the bag when I received it – a great pity.

The assumed handkerchief actually turned out to be a 'fabric envelope' to contain stockings or underwear etc. The fabric was placed right side down and the two sides folded in towards the centre; the two remaining corners were folded in and the loop attached to the pearl button on the top of the crown. The lace writing was then on the underside of the 'envelope'. On closer examination it has also been found that the lettering was, not Honiton rib as described, but a lace braid with a double footside. I have also discovered from evidence given to Dr Stewart in 1841, for the Employment of Children Report of 1843, that what I originally called the sachet was, in fact, "the Queen's work-bag, which was worked in gold". I have therefore assumed that the other metallic lace edging also used gold thread as the gimp and not silver as I originally assumed. What a pity it has tarnished over the years; I am sure it would have gleamed.

In the following pages of the book I have answered many questions but others remain unanswered, so – the work into this lost lace will need to continue. Penderel Moody wrote in her book of 1909, 'Lacemaking and Collecting', that "there is plenty of research work waiting for the lace historians"[1] – I now know what she meant!!

2   *Devon Trolly Lace*

What is Devon Trolly Lace?

Many of the historical books studied defined Devon Trolly Lace as resembling many of the continuous laces made in the Midlands at the present time. It was made of a coarse British thread, with heavy bobbins and worked on – round and round the pillow, having taken its origin from the Flemish 'Trolle Kant', where the design was outlined with a thick cordonnet thread, the design and grounding net being worked in conjunction with each other.   For example, in Pillow and Point Lace, Mary Sharpe quotes "Early Devonshire lace appears, however, sometimes to have one peculiarity distinguishing it from both Brussels and from the later Honiton. It is the use of an outlining 'cordonnet' or 'trolly' or gimp, from which it was known as Trolly Lace. The development of this lace has followed much the same course as did those of Flanders"[2] and N. Hudson Moore quotes that "The name 'Trolly lace' has been transferred to England, and given to a class of laces with grounds which resemble the Flemish 'Trolle Kant' grounds, and which have a thick thread cordonnet".[3]

Old Flemish (Trolle Kant)

There is, however, much more detailed additional information to these generalised definitions.

Mrs Palliser in her 1st edition of 1865 states "The term 'Trolly' appears now to be applied in Devonshire to narrow pillow laces, whether of double or single ground" and "the ground double so similar to that of the Flanders laces, from which country it doubtless derives it name". [4] In her 2nd edition of 1869 she states that "it is impossible to get a clear definition of the term"[5] but in the reprint of 1902 she states "it may be derived from a corruption of French 'toile' applied to distinguish a flat linen pattern from the ground 'treille', a general term for net ground... It is now almost extinct in

Devonshire, remaining in the hands of the Midland counties where it more properly belongs"[6] – she obviously kept changing her mind, going from a precise definition to a possible one!

Yallop, in 'The History of the Honiton Lace Industry' says that "Trolly lace is a straight lace and is, therefore, different in the technique of making from the free lace of the Honiton industry". [7] Hudson-Moore states that "the Trolly lace is distinguished by having a heavier looking thread in various parts of the pattern. This is always made by twisting threads of the bobbins together, never by the introduction of a coarse thread".[8] In studying the samples of Trolly lace in the bag and those in the lace collections of Exeter Museum, I did not find one sample whereby this statement was proven; all samples had separate cordonnet threads. I noted with amusement that, in an article for Cassell's Family Magazine in 1893 and entitled 'With the Devonshire Lace-makers', Edith Long Fox published the following illustration as 'Ancient Honiton'!

Mrs Neville Jackson states that "Devonshire Trolly lace was made with the English thread of a coarser quality than that of Flanders",[9] while Penderel Moody informs the reader that "The Trolly lace of Devon and Suffolk was very similar, in both cases keeping closely to the same Flemish origin. The decoration consisted of rings outlined with a heavy gimp thread and the lace took its name from the number of rings and holes".[10] Bullock adds the information that "all the early Flemish laces required a large number of bobbins and had very intricate patterns".[11] This statement is certainly true of the wider complex Trolly designs contained within the bag.

Caulfield & Saward, in 'The Dictionary of Needlework', define Trolly Lace as "pillow laces, made in Normandy, in Flanders, in Buckinghamshire and Devonshire. The distinguishing feature of these laces is their ground which is an imitation of the Antwerp Trolly Net or Point de Paris Ground and is made with twists while the pattern is outlined with a thick thread like that used in the old Flemish laces known as Trolle Kant".[12] "The ground was a six-pointed star reseau, or fond chant, the lace was worked round and round the pillow. The name was probably derived from the Flemish 'Trolle Kant'".[13]

The introduction of Trolly Lace into Devonshire

The numerous references to the words 'Flanders' and 'Flemish', in the quotes given, must surely indicate a link between that lace-making area and Devon. Many books refer to the 'industrious Flemings' who introduced lace making into Devon, and some indicate that the Flemings 'improved' the lace making skills already known to the County. Thomas Wright, writing in 'Romance to the Lace Pillow', states that "While however the Valencienne workers drifted to Cranfield, those from Normandy made their way to Devonshire, where they introduced the Trolly lace industry".[14] He continues that "Others escaped by sea, putting out from Havre, Nantes, la Rochelle and Bordeaux in trading ships, shallops, fishing smacks, open boats – any wretched werry…..others were landed with wounded skins, but with whole and merry consciences at Southampton, Dartmouth and Plymouth".[15] These statements may give us an indication of the time that Trolly lace first appeared in Devon as the Refugees from Normandy came to England in 1685 and Celia Fiennes, writing in her diary of 1698 wrote, "here (Honiton) they make fine Bone lace in imitation of the Antwerp and Flanders lace".[16] Also Pamela Sharpe, in her meticulously researched book on Colyton, spoke of the Pinney family who were lace dealers, writing that "The Pinneys seemed to be all but out of the trade by the 1700s as the fashion turned away from Honiton lace to Bedfordshire and Buckinghamshire lighter laces".[17] Some of the fourth influx of refugees from the French Revolution of 1789 also made their way to Devon, but there is no evidence, from either text or samples, so far available, that the Revolution Lace pattern made in Northamptonshire and illustrated in Thomas Wright's 'Romance to the Lace Pillow, in Plate 13, was also made in Devon.

Palliser wrote that "The origin of Trolly was undoubtedly Flemish, but it is said to have reached Devonshire at the time of the French Revolution, through the Normandy peasants, driven by want of employment from their own country, where lace was a great industry during the 18thC".[18] She further writes "We may rather infer that laces of silk and coarse thread were already fabricated in Devonshire as elsewhere, and that the Flemings, on their arrival having introduced a fine thread, then spun almost exclusively in their own country, from that period the trade of bone-lace making flourished in the southern as in the Midland counties of England".[19]

Santina Levey states that "It has been suggested that the term 'trolly' (or trolle) was a corruption of the West Flanders word *drol*, meaning coarse thread, or of the Brussels-Flemish word *trolies*, meaning the bars used to ground a lace. The former is more likely as it was used in Flanders to describe a coarse Mechlin style lace with a heavy cordonnet and it is likely that it was this type of lace that the refugee lace-makers brought with them to England".[20]

John Yallop supports these theories as he could find no evidence that Trolly Lace was introduced from the Midlands, including the fact that Devon had no lace chants, tells or songs which were common in the Buckinghamshire lace area at the time. However the Parish Registers for East Devon clearly show a connection between France, the Channel Islands and East Devon in the early years of the industry. In studying the Census returns for 1851, as no places of birth were given on the 1841 Census, I was surprised at the number of lace makers who would have been making lace in the early years of the 19th century, who were born outside the East Devon area, but in other lace making centres and probably came to East Devon on their marriage, to seafaring men.

Yallop also suggests that the smuggling routes from France to Beer and Seaton may have been the means for some French lace makers entering the County and settling in the area.

Lace-makers on the 1851 Census born outside East Devon				
Dublin	2		Jersey	2
France	1 – Brit. Subj.		Scotland	1
Guernsey	2		Suffolk	1
Hampshire	3		The Hague	1
Isle of Wight	2		Yorkshire	1

Travellers of the time, writing their travel memoirs, mention the lace industry and the types of lace made. Fuller, writing in his 'Worthies of England', praised the Devon lace Industry….. "The lace makers of Devon, in the 17thC made fabrics rivalling those of the Low Countries. The Trolly Lace also made in the South West rivalled the Flemish varieties, although worked with a coarser thread." [21]

Who, where and when?

Who?

According to Bury Palliser, Trolly Lace "was not the work of women alone. In the flourishing days of its manufacture, every boy, until he attained the age of fifteen, and was competent to work in the fields, attended the lace schools daily. A lace-maker at Sidmouth, verging on thirty-five, learned her craft at the village dame school, in company with many boys. The men, especially the sailor returned from sea, would again resume the employment of boyhood, in their hours of leisure, and the labourer, seated at his pillow on a summer's evening would add to his weekly gains".[22]

She also informs the reader that Captain Marryat, the brother of Mrs Bury Palliser, succeeded "in finding out a man of sixty, in James Gooding, dweller in Salcombe parish, near Sidmouth, who had in his day been a lace-maker of some reputation. 'I have made hundreds of yards in my time' he said 'both wide and narrow, but never worked regularly at my pillow after sixteen years of age.' Delighted to exhibit the craft of his boyhood, he hunted out his patterns, and setting to work, produced a piece of trolly edging, which soon found a place in the albums of sundry lace collecting ladies, the last specimen of man-worked lace likely to be fabricated in the county of Devon".[23]   On the 1851 Census James Gooding is recorded as being an unmarried, 45 year old gardener.

Mrs Treadwin, Palliser's contemporary informed her that, "in her younger days, saw some twenty-four men lacemakers in her native village of Woodbury, two of whom, Palmer by name, were still surviving in 1869, and one of these worked at his pillow so late as 1820".[24] She does not state which type of lace that they made, but there is the possibility that it could have been Trolly lace. Both Palliser and Wright mention men making Trolly lace, but I could find no primary evidence to support this fact from available records, as the only reference to male lace-makers living in the coastal area on the 1841 and 1851 Census' were:

1841	James Jenkins	20	Beer	)	these three men
	Robert Harding	13	Branscombe	)	must have moved
	George Rendle	27	Littleham	)	to other jobs by 1851
1851	John Newton	17	Beer		
	Thomas Bramfield	9	Branscombe		
	Robert Perriman	15	"		
	John Perriman	12	"		
	John Acland	65	Littleham	Pauper lace-maker & not recorded on the 1841 census as a lace-maker.	
	John Vinicombe	6m	Otterton	an enumerators error?!	

which implies that the male lace-makers were producing Trolly Lace much earlier than records show, if these statements are correct, and why should we doubt them?

The evidence for the House of Commons Report on the Employment of Children, gathered from primary sources by Dr Stewart in 1841, contains several references to Trolly Lace being made:

Betty Hart, daughter of Sarah Hart from Otterton, the oldest scholar in Mrs Roger's Lace School at Sidmouth was "out of her time at learning 'head work' or 'Honiton work' in a year and a half, but she had before learned Trolly work for 12 months at Otterton".[25] The report also stated that Betty could read the Bible and Testament and went to the Church Sunday school, but could not write.

Mary Ann Rogers, mistress of the principal Lace School in Sidmouth, "learned Trolly work at seven years old at Lympstone; this is edging, and is easier than the 'head work' or the 'sprigs and flowers'.[26] Mary was seven in 1811 when she would have been learning to make lace.

In Newton Poppleford, the report states Mary Gooding aged 14, "Learned of Sarah Tovey for a year to do Trolly which is for borders. It is 'yard work' that is, paid by the yard. Can now do Trolly very well and earn 3d a day". [27] Mary could read the Bible and Testament and write her name. Elizabeth Newbury, also from the same village, aged "near twenty-one" and "Mrs Rice's eldest girl" informed Dr Stewart that "the Trolly is sooner learned than the 'head work', but is not quite so well paid".[28] Mrs Rice ran one of the Lace Schools in the village.

Jourdain states that an informant, writing from East Budleigh in 1896, said that "some of the very old women here make beautiful Trolly lace but no young person. This is partly owing to there being no prickings left, for one of the old workers told me that when the lace trade was bad they used the prickings as stiffening for their waist belts, thinking they should never need them again".[29]

Of the 947 entries on the 1841 Census for the East Devon lace-making area, concerning lace related employment, there are 22 entries recorded as

Lace Dealers(5)	Lace Sewers(2)
Lace Manufacturers(2)	Lace Apprentices (11)
Lace Representatives(2)	

Of the remaining entries only Mary Perriam 25, of Littleham, Eliza Eavens 30, of Otterton and Sarah Priddis 20, of Sidmouth specify that they are 'sprig makers'. It is therefore impossible to ascertain the percentage of lace-makers producing Trolly Lace as opposed to Honiton lace at the time. It is interesting to note that in Maria Hutchins evidence, of 1841, to Dr Stewart she "States that there are at least 100 women and children about Woodbury Salterton working at 'lace-making'",[30] but the Census enumerator for 1841 only recorded three lacemakers, namely, Triphena Richards aged 40, Sarah Rowland aged 60 and Agnes Stamp, aged 55 and living next to 'Basses', Woodbury Salterton. However, 10 years later the 1851 Census records the following lace-makers who would have been old enough to be making or learning to make lace in 1841; the two lace dealer/manufacturers recorded, suggests that lace making was a very prolific and established industry in the village.

1851 Census – Woodbury Salterton Lacemakers

Name	Age	Status		Husband's occupation
Elizabeth Bond	42	m		Agricultural worker
Sarah Bond	18	u		
Mary Calloway	68	m	Pauper	Pauper
Mary Carter	47	w		
Margaret Crewes	23	m		Agricultural worker
Harriet Dart	24	u		
Johanna Easterbrook	64	w		Lace Traveller
Jane Mary England	23	m		Brick / tile maker
Lina Furse	27	m		Carpenter
Ann Hanley	27	u		
Sarah Havill	57	m		Agricultural worker
Mary Hearn	22	u*		
Charlotte Hitchock	39	m		Agricultural worker
Jessy Howe	20	u		
Sarah Lavis	66	m	Pauper	Pauper
Eleanor Lavis	30	m		Agricultural worker
Sarah Marks	27	u		
Elizabeth Moore	76	w		
Sarah Moore	59	m		Agricultural worker
Mary Norrish	77	w		Lace Traveller
Ann Potter	20	u		
Aiset Pyle	47	m		Agricultural worker
Elizabeth Shepherd	26	m		Shoemaker
Jane Shepherd	38	u		
Susan Skinner	32	m		Agricultural worker
Elizabeth Skinner	47	m		Agricultural worker
Eliza Skinner	20	u		
Wilmet Skinner	38	m		Agricultural worker
Agnes Stamp	66	w		
Mary Ann Stamp	36	u		
Elizabeth Stamp	31	m		Agricultural worker
Anna Street	21	u		
Mary Taylor	60	nk	Pauper	
Mary Ann Taylor	21	u		
Elizabeth Turl	41	m		Agricultural worker
Sarah Ware	18	u		
Sarah Webber	40	m		Cordwainer
Sarah Ann Wilson	28	m		Agricultural worker
James Clarke	56			Lace Manufacturer
Mary Phillips	37	m		Lace dealer

m=married   u=unmarried   w=widow

*   Mary Hearn 's name is written on the reverse of one of the paper sheets contained in the bag. She had a sister, Asenath, aged 13 in 1851, who was also a lace maker.

The 1851 Census also records Cecilia Barrett, Mary Ann Barrett, Jane Barrett, Caroline Davey, Mary Ann German, Charlotte Grant, Mary Ann Taylor as sprigmakers, with Eliza Hutchings and Ann Wilde as 'Lace Pointers'. This gives evidence that both Trolly and Honiton lace were being made simultaneously in the village. It is also interesting to note that Elizabeth Turl, 41, is recorded as a lace- maker in 1851, a Lace Manufacturer in 1861 and as a Honiton lace-maker in 1871; was she making Trolly lace prior to transferring her skills to Honiton lace? – we shall never know.

Where?

Defoe, writing in 1724, recorded that "the lace manufacture extended from Exmouth to Torbay...",[31] however we cannot ascertain whether this statement applied to lace-making in general or was only applicable to Trolly lace.

The Revd. Gidley, Vicar of Branscombe, in his letter of 1820, wrote "The lace makers along the coast continue to make an inferior lace of British thread, called Trolly lace, of which they sell great quantities".[32] Gidley's letter is the earliest known reference to the making of this form of lace in Devon and, although his wording suggests an established technique, it seems possible that it was not of long standing, especially since its location was in a restricted part only of the Honiton lace making area. The question arises, therefore, of how this manufacture, which had been carried on elsewhere, in Flanders, Normandy and the East Midlands at least, for some two centuries, came to the East Devon coastal villages.

The 1850 White's Trade Directory refers to "an inferior kind of lace, made of British thread, in the villages along the coast is called Trolly lace".[33]

Mrs Head, in her book ' The Lace and Embroidery Collector – A Guide to Old Lace & Embroidery', wrote that Trolly Lace "had a certain popularity in the eighteenth century, but it's production, which was chiefly in the district around Exmouth, has long ceased in Devonshire, although a lace not dissimilar is still made in the Midlands".[34] That "Thirteen-hole Trolly was obtainable in the villages round Exmouth, but the industry is now practically extinct" was a fact presented in many late 19th and early 20th century books.

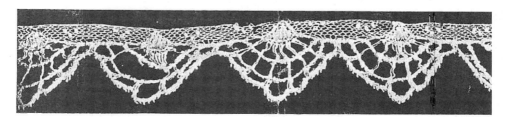

Thirteen-hole Trolly, made near Exmouth as late as 1896

The only other specified village in diaries and text is Otterton, where Polwhele, a historian in 1790 wrote the the "females of the village are entirely manufacturers of a coarse kind of thread lace".[35] In the evidence for the Employment of Children survey, 1841, Beer, Exmouth, Lympstone, Newton Poppleford, and Sidmouth are mentioned for making Trolly lace, but surprisingly although there is evidence from lace makers in Woodbury and Woodbury Salterton, reference to the making of Trolly Lace is omitted.; was this because they assumed that everyone was making it and therefore to mention it specifically was of little consequence?

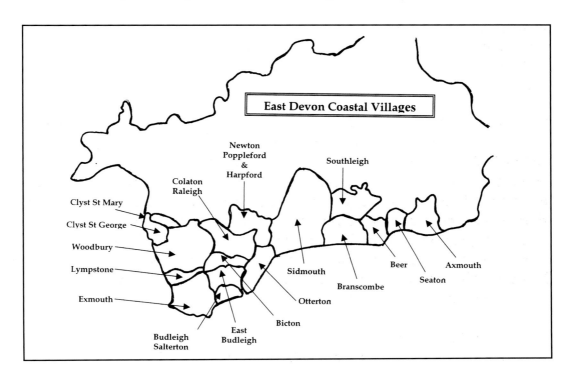

When?

Palliser, in her 1st edition of 1865 states that "Much Trolly lace was made in Devonshire until 30 years back, when the fabric was unmercifully overthrown".[36] This would indicate that Trolly Lace was made until approximately 1835 when "the caprices of fashion, combined with the physician's decree, which banished from the nursery those lace trimmed caps which so much added to the beauty of the new born infant".[37] This statement links with the comment on a page of Trolly patterns in Mrs Treadwin's Lace Sample book that they were 'made in Woodbury as late as 1840'.

Numerical information acquired and calculations made from the 'Employment of Children Report', 1841, inform us that Mary Ann Rogers learned to make Trolly lace at 7, in 1811 and that Eleanor Rice, aged 48 of Newton Poppleford began the art of Trolly at the age of 5 or 6 in 1798/9, whilst Mary Driver, 30 of Beer learned Trolly at the age of 6 in 1819. This gives primary evidence to an established Trolly Lace industry during the late 18th century.

Fuller, Feines and Sharpe all mention Trolly Lace being made during the early 1700s and this evidence would match with some locally owned and dated Trolly bobbins. Santina Levey gives a contextual summary of Trolly Lace, with it "being made in England in the late 17thC onwards. In the mid 18thC, when it appears to have been a light silk or thread lace of the Blonde type, it was made in both Devon and the Midland Counties. By the 19thC, it is a coarse straight lace made in Devon, although the Midland County workers still called the heavy gimp bobbins 'Trollies' ".[38] She also writes that "The English industry does seem to have been hit by the changing styles of the second quarter of the century; it was less easy for it to produce the delicately-patterned lace in which the net ground was beginning to play an important part".[39]

The Report of the Juries for the Great Exhibition of 1851 state that "Pillow' or 'Thread lace' although made upon the cushion like the Honiton lace, is distinguished from it by having both the pattern and the mesh made by the hand, whereas in Honiton lace, the pattern is made separately and afterwards sewn on to machine net."[40]

The 1861 Census records all the lace-makers of Beer as 'Honiton lace-makers' and since it is known from the Children's Employment evidence that Trolly Lace was made in the fishing village in 1841 and earlier, one can correctly assume that it's production, in Beer, had ceased by 1861.

In the Transactions of the Bath & West of England Agricultural Society, its meeting in 1876, held at Hereford, records "The specimens of Honiton and

Devonshire Trolly lace submitted in competition for the prizes so liberally given by J.C. Moore Stevens Esq. of Winscott Norton, Devon deserve very high commendation".[41] Also in the Bath & West of England Society (V&A) 1879 catalogue, Section 461 was won by Elizabeth Phillips for producing 1 ½ yards of Trolly Lace. She won £1-15-00 for her efforts at the age of 48, no doubt a useful addition to the family income, her husband being a farmer at Heathfield Farm, which is equidistant from Woodbury and Woodbury Salterton. There is no mention of Trolly Lace in Catalogues after 1880.

Penderel Moody, writing in 1907, says that "several nets have been revived in Devon of late years, but the favoured one is Trolly, which is the same as Buckinghamshire. The net may be the same, but the patterns are very different".[42]

What equipment was required to make Trolly lace?

Bobbins

There appears to be a difference between the Trolly bobbins of the Midland areas and of Devonshire. Thomas Wright states that "in Buckinghamshire a Trolly bobbin was the bobbin onto which the gimp thread was wound from the quill; it usually had pewter gingles. In Huntingdonshire the trollies were known as 'Bedfordshire Trailers'".[43] The Trolly bobbins of Devonshire were larger than Honiton lace sticks and had blunt ends, according to both Jourdain and Bullock, but Wright states that "Honiton Trolly bobbins have also the two necks, but no examples of this type have been found".[44]

The search for Devon Trolly bobbins has been extensive and produced very few examples of note. Local lace colleagues have now identified the mysterious bobbin or bobbins that they have had in their collections and only five have been purchased since the research began. It is interesting to note how few are available compared to the numerous antique Honiton bobbins – where have they all gone? Were they simply disposed of when the making of Trolly Lace ended or were they perhaps whittled down to make another Honiton bobbin as a form of re-cycling? We shall never know, although Lillie Trivett remembers using some Trolly bobbins when learning to make lace in Colyton Primary School in the late 1930s.

3 design motifs from a Trolly bobbin

I commissioned a set of twenty-four Trolly bobbins from Geoff Downs, well known in the lace world as 'Itsa Bobbins', so that I could try to make a complete pattern using just Trolly bobbins. I chose Geoff to make the bobbins as I had discovered, through talking to him, that he had attended Woodbury Salterton Primary School; as a young boy he never knew that the bag of lace was in the attic above the classroom where he undertook his studies!! I worked Pattern PG7, see page 52 and found that the size of the bobbins was too great to make working the lace a pleasant experience, even on such a narrow edging, or was I just not used to using such heavy bobbins? From this experiment I deduced that the Trolly bobbins were probably used purely to identify the gimp thread and that the lace makers would have used their Honiton bobbins to make the Trolly patterns, as the majority of us have done in working the redrawn samples. This assumption would also perhaps explain why fewer Devon Trolly bobbins have been found.

After having made that assumption I then discovered an undated 'Weldon's Practical Needlework' (No.229, Vol.20) magazine, the front cover showing a bolster pillow, with a pricking that went 'round and round' and Devon Trolly bobbins, being used in their entirety.

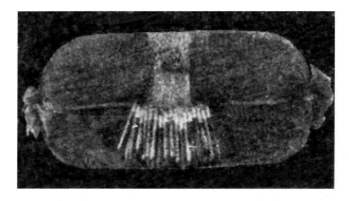

scanned from Weldon's front cover

The photo also showed a Point Ground edging and was taken by G.H. Barton of Seaton, Devon, so one may assume that he used local equipment for the photograph. Now I am undecided as to how the Trolly bobbins were used – shades of Mrs Palliser, I think!

Palliser, when referring to lace being made in Devonshire, wrote "This explanation (referring to the use of fish bones as pins) would seem more probable than that of employing sheep's trotters for bobbins, which as from 300-400 bobbins are often used on a pillow, must have been both heavy and burdensome".[44] The mind boggles at this image, but if we are realistic and think or assume that she is referring to Trolly Lace rather than Honiton lace, for which this number of bobbins would not be required, then the use of Trolly bobbins for the whole piece of lace would, indeed, be burdensome.

Thread

There are many references to a 'coarse thread' being used to make Devonshire Trolly Lace. Yallop produced a comparative Table of Threads and their uses which supports this theory. The threads ranged from '105 and '140' for a "coarser type of lace" to '500' which was "the finest ever used".[46] However, the majority of the pattern samples that follow, in the Pattern Section, were made in 120/2 thread, hardly coarse by today's, standards, but perhaps by comparison to the very fine thread being used to make Honiton lace in earlier times, the correct adjective.

C.R.Clifford stated in 'The Lace Dictionary', that "Trolly lace was made with its English thread of coarser quality than Flemish thread",[47] whilst Mrs Lowes, in her 'Chats on Old Lace and Needlework' used the word coarse to define the gimp thread. "Most of the old Devonshire laces bear distinct likeness to the Flemish laces, only the clumsiness of the design or the coarse workmanship differentiating them. It has, however, one special feature which gave it the name 'Trolly lace', as unlike, the perfectly flat lace of Flanders, it has a coarse thread or 'trolly' outlining its patterns and being made of English thread is not very durable".[48]

Prickings

As already stated the prickings had been used for stiffening waistbands and it is a great pity that there were no samples of the old Trolly prickings available to study, in the bag. However, during research at the Royal Albert Memorial Museum, two pricking samples of Pattern PG73 were found. According to Jourdain "some old trolly prickings leave the net unpricked as in one class of Valencienne lace"[49] but this was not the case of the PG73 prickings – every pin hole in the net had been worked.

Pillows

There is also no evidence of the type of pillow used to make Trolly Lace, however the phrase 'working round and round' the pillow, suggests a Midlands bolster type pillow. In 'An Elementary Course for Lacemaking' by Winser, the authors write that "The different Trolly-laces – the patterns of which are worked in the length by being rolled round the cushion in a continuous band—such as borders, insertions, etc., are made on a bolster-shaped cushion, and worked from the front only, the bobbins being laid back on the sides, and the finished lace rolled up at the back as it is worked (*see Fig. 43*).[45] Note the style of bobbins being used, a combination of Honiton and other unspangled bobbins, that are not Devon Trollys. The pattern being worked appears to be Torchon .

Fig. 43—Torchon Pillow or Cushion.

We have worked the pattern samples using small and very large Honiton pillows, rectangular domed pillows and modern circular pillows, both flat and slightly raised; on all, except the Honiton pillow, it proved difficult to control the Honiton bobbins in the large quantities required for some of the patterns. Some lace makers resorted to using their Midland type bobbins as the sheer quantity of Honiton bobbins proved too difficult to manage.

How was Trolly lace used?

Francis Kirkham of Devon, in his inventory of 1677, included "1 cravat and cuffs of Trolly lace 2s 6d".[51] This appears to be the first mention of Trolly Lace, although we do not know the country of origin, but the date would support the earlier quotes of Fuller and Feines.

Santina Levey suggests that "the narrow strips of lace were joined to make quite large items, like hooded capes, worn by women in the middle of the 18thC".[52] Mrs Delaney's sister, Mrs Dewes, may have meant such a hooded cape when she wrote to an acquaintance "I fancy her friend, Mrs Egerton has *vamped her up* with a *trollyhood* and a fashionable negligee etc."[53]

Several authors gave the following example: 'Lappets and scarfs were made of Trolly lace from an early date'. Mrs Delaney,in one of her letters, dated 1756, speaks of a 'Trolly head' and "Trolly lace, before its downfall, has been sold at the extravagant price of five guineas a yard.".[54] She also reported to her sister that "the ruffles are much the same as at Bath, long at the elbow and pretty narrow at the top;...heads are variously adorned, pompoms with some accompaniment of feathers, ribbons or flowers; lappets in all sorts of curlis murlis; little plain cypress gauze, *trolly* or fine muslin"[55]

Possible uses for Trolly Lace, as it was generally described as a 'trimming lace', could have been on berthas, bibs, capes, coifs, collars, cuffs, dresses, chemises, evening gowns, fans, fichus, flounces, hankies, bonnets, headwear, lappets, veils and bonnet veils, parasols, petticoats, ruffs, wrist ruffs, shawls and wedding clothes for the highly fashionable ladies. Bib-fronted bands, cravats, cuffs, hankies, ruffs, shirts and sleeves for the men and on all kind of baby clothes for infants. Many historical lace and fashion books refer to Trolly lace trimming babies caps, bonnets, underclothing and collars.

William Connor Sydney, writing about the English in the 18th century, states that "Lace ruffles were commonly worn by gentlemen as ornaments for the neck".[56] In the reign of Anne two lace cravats "were considered enough for any young gentleman of quality. In 1751, the Earl of Chesterfield in writing to his son, bade him bring with him only two or three of his laced shirts. Point ruffles graced the hands of beaux till the close of the century".[57] Twice the newspapers in 1780 recorded that during the Gordon Riots a report was circulated through the metropolis that the Earl of Effingham, who had joined the rioters, had been mortally wounded, and that his body, which had been thrown into the River Thames had been recognised by the lace ruffles he wore". Were they Trolly Lace ruffles?

There is also an interesting account of lace being stolen from a shop in Devon for use on a mob-cap. From the lengths of lace mentioned, it may be correctly assumed that it was Trolly Lace.

10 May 1819
Information and complaint of Sarah Weymouth Southwood, spinster of Dodbrook:
She is aged 12 ½ and attends in the shop of her aunt, Susannah Goodman in Kingsbridge, where is sold linen drapery and lace. On the 4th of May Sarah was tending the shop while her aunt was absent ill, when Ann Bate, the wife of George Bate, tailor of Kingsbridge, came in and asked to see some lace. Sarah showed her all the thread lace her aunt had. Bate asked if she could take four pieces of thread lace to show a lady for whom she was making a mob-cap. The four pieces were marked in yards; one was 5 yds, another 10 yds, another 11 yds and the fourth 2 yds. She had seen her aunt measure off two of the pieces and she had measured the other two and was sure none had been sold since the measuring. Ann Bate returned the lace in less than an hour saying that the lady liked the lace but would wait until the aunt was recovered as she thought the aunt would sell it cheaper. Sarah thought the lace looked smaller, and two days later re-measured them and found that 1 ½ yds was missing from the 5 yd piece, 3 yds was missing from the 11 yd piece and 3 ½ yds was missing from the 10 yd piece, but none from the small piece. Ann Bate was sent for and said "Oh my dear I have been using some lace to put on my old caps and I will go and see if it is amongst them". She returned in five minutes saying, "here my dear, here is the widest lace, and as God is my only saviour and judge, I did not know it was there". The piece returned was 1 ½ yds, but when Bate carried the 5 yd piece from the shop it was uncut. She did not know what had happened to the narrow lace, but taking a shawl from the window and shaking it about cried, "Oh my dear, there it is, there it is". This informant though saw nothing falling from the shawl, but Ann pointed with her foot at something on the ground and said, "what is that?" And then putting down her hand took from the floor, as if had just fallen there, 3 ½ yds of each sort of lace missing, adding "don't you tell, there is a good child, and I'll come tomorrow and join in for you". On Saturday last Bate came to the shop and said she knew how the narrow lace came there, and then she conversed with Sarah's mother, who was then present, while Sarah went to the door as there were persons looking at some goods on the outside. She believes the missing lace was feloniously embezzled by Ann Bate.[58]

When attending the Christmas Lacemakers Fair 2003 at the NEC in Birmingham, I was fortunate to be given some copies of Bonhams Auctioneer catalogues, containing samples of lace, textiles and needlework ephemera. In the December 2002 catalogue there is a photograph of Lot 760 showing Amelia Margareta Dixon, (1756-1841) from Holton Hall 'dripping' in lace that could, with the artists' license, be one of the first Devon Trolly Lace patterns that was reworked. My excitement on seeing this portrait, made my journey home to Devon a much more pleasant experience! The portrait, attributed to Benjamin Hudson shows Amelia holding a Filet bodkin and measuring stick; does this mean that she was a lace-maker or were the implements for effect? I like to think the former is true. See p. 45

Palliser writes that "In 1763, that 'neat shop near the Stinking Style, in Lukenbooths', held by Mr James Baillie, advertises 'Trollies, English laces and pearl edgings'".[59] Does this mean that the Trolly Lace was of foreign extract?

On searching various English and American newspapers, advertising features or announcements showed that Trolly Lace was 'in fashion'. In the Boston Gazette & Country Journal, 1774, Samual Parkman from his shop in Union Street, was selling "… a great variety of black & white Bone, Blond & Trolly laces and edging", which had been imported by ship from London and Glasgow.   Mr Parkman "asks the Favour of those who have Money to lay out to call and see him, that he may have an Opportunity to prove to them that his Goods are really 'very cheap'".   M. Lee was also selling "White – a large variety of trolly", from his shop in Newbury Street but as it does not specify that this lace was imported, it may have been the product from the Lace Industry of Ipswich, Massachussetts.

Mrs Treadwin was still advertising Trolly Lace in an 1886 edition of the Devon & Exeter Daily Gazette, so presumably it was either still being made by a few lace makers or she was trying to sell old stock!

Financial matters – the cost and payments

It is fortunate that the lace samples in the Dealer's bag are nearly all priced per yard, either by an attached small square ticket on the Queen's sampler, or hand written on the sample pages of paper and fabric. The price per yard ranges from 2 ½ d for the narrowest braid to 12 shillings per yard for the most complex. By today's standards that is £1-09 to £63-03 based on 1750 prices and by comparison one needed 3d to get drunk, 6d to get very drunk! 13s 6d to buy a yard of Mechlin lace and 16s to buy a pair of ruffles. For £6-00 a gentleman could have a night out in London, a good meal, a bath and a fashionable courtesan; today that would equate to £639-00!!   The prices for the same lace vary on different page samples, but I could not understand the pricing system as patterns of some complexity were priced below those of simpler patterns and there was no correlation of price due to the width of the pattern; perhaps demand for a particular pattern determined the price.

Much has been reported in other books of the oppressive 'truck system' that operated in the lace-making areas. It is good to know though that Miss Pidsley, the benefactor of Woodbury Salterton village, "always pays money, which she, Mrs Hutchins thinks a very great advantage; as it is generally found that in exchange for goods they do not get more than the value of ninepence, or even eightpence, out of a shilling; and if it is even paid in money, there is always a deduction made of threepence out of every shilling".[60]

There are however, some interesting comments from the 'English Women's Domestic Magazine' of 1866 when a review was made of the newly published 'History of Lace' by Mrs Palliser. The unnamed reviewer writes "as to the prospects of the lace trade in this country, they certainly do not, judging from Mrs Bury Palliser's book, seem very brilliant. Of many places in England where it was formerly made in large quantities, we find it stated that 'the whole of the lace trade has died out', while throughout Scotland it has declined altogether. Nor is this state of things to be much regretted if the information is quite correct concerning those places where it is still made – namely that 'a good lace-maker may earn from tenpence to one shilling per day'. But in this, it is to be hoped, there may be a trifling mistake, as it is not pleasant to reflect that of the large prices given for English lace so small a sum finds it way to the persons engaged in the arduous work of making it and so great a profit to the dealers. It can scarcely be agreeable to a lady purchasing or wearing any of the beautiful specimens exhibited in the London shops to contemplate the poor lace-makers bending from morning to night over her weary task for tenpence day".[61] One would like to think that these sentiments, although expressed after the demise of the Trolly Lace industry, were applicable during it's heyday, but in reality I doubt that those purchasing the expensive lace would have given it much thought.

We have no way of knowing the percentage of the retail prices that the lacemaker's were paid for their efforts, but as the lace-makers of Woodbury Salterton were referred to, in the 1841 Times newspaper, as 'destitute' it was obviously a pittance.

The worked pattern samples in the book all have their original price and today's equivalent for comparison; perhaps you could assess your potential earnings at today's prices, I know I did and soon realised that I would certainly have been as destitute as they were in times gone by if I was being paid by the yard!

The patterns and their comparison to other Trolly laces

One of the first tasks required for making such a comparison was to categorise the 726 lace samples in the bag. As there were no names to any patterns, or prickings giving pattern numbers, some form of identification was necessary. After some false starts I finally decided on the classification system that is explained at the introduction to the pattern section.

My first foray was to study the Devon Trolly patterns accumulated by Mrs Palliser and Mrs Treadwin and held in their collections in the Royal Albert Memorial Museum, Exeter. There were 92 samples of Devonshire Trolly Lace, in these two collections, with which to compare the Woodbury Salterton lace patterns. Only 10 samples were an exact match.

Penderel Moody in 1907 writes that "With the revival of Trolly lace in the Midlands many of the regular Devon patterns have been re-named as Buckinghamshire, and it is difficult to say with absolute conviction where the difference came in. Devon had one very inexpensive Trolly pattern, which is unlike any Midland lace, but is closely related to Suffolk." This pattern is known locally as 'Blowbrain', "where the pattern is a collection of small holes, arranged to form a scallop and finished with only two or three rows of narrow net above."[62] Whilst it looks like Bucks Point Honeycombe, it consists of W.S. and 3 twists before the pin and the same after the pin. The grid is 60 degrees. The footside is worked on the left, the Continental way. The late Mrs Marjorie Tolhurst (Devon Lace Teacher) told Ada Archer and Mary de Salis, (her then pupils and now both Devon Lace Teachers) that there was only one remaining pattern of Devon Trolley Lace, 'Blowbrain', so named because it was put round caps, i.e. 'below the brain'! This version was also told to me by Lillie Trivett, who kindly supplied me with the pattern and instructions and although this folk lore is well known in Devon, of its validity I know not.

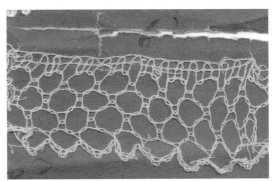

Sample of Blow Brain

Penderel Moody continued to say of Devon Trolly Lace that "the general effect was poor, and the patterns not worth reviving. Other Trolly patterns which may still be found in the cottages are of much better lace, but not in any way distinctive".[63] I would have to take issue with this statement now that the bag of Trolly Lace samples has come to light. Many of the patterns in the bag, and indeed in the Royal Albert Memorial Museum, Exeter are very distinctive and extremely complex in design, requiring a large number of bobbins and having several gimp threads to form the pattern. Even the most symmetrical and geometric patterns, when studied and worked have some peculiarities in them that would tax the modern lace-maker. It is interesting to note that a book published in 1936 quotes "Specimens are very rare indeed".[64] Fortunately due to the 'find' this is no longer the case.

Penderel Moody also states that "The stitches of Queen Katherine and of the Lille workers are not to be found in Devon Trolly, and the similarity to Suffolk would lead one to suppose the lace took its origin from some Flemish designs not extant".[65] Now that the recently discovered samples can be studied, there are several whose ground is constructed in Kat Stitch and if the Lille workers, used *fond chant* as their ground stitch, then the Devon Trolly samples fully comply with this method of working the ground.

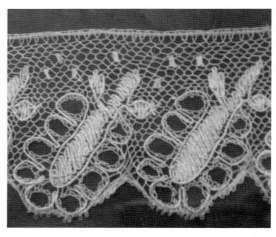

Two samples of Suffolk lace with the permission of the Victoria &Albert Museum

Pat Earnshaw describes the Devon Trolly patterns as having "a simple and homely charm".[66] I wonder whether Queen Victoria thought they were 'simple and homely' when selecting from the sampler? I wish we knew what the five samples that she chose looked like as I assume that the gaps, on the sampler, contained the patterns that she chose to be made by the lace makers of Woodbury Salterton.

In Palliser's 4th edition of 1902, mention was made of Ripon, in Yorkshire. "At what period, and by whom the lace manufacture of Ripon was founded, we have been unable to ascertain. It was probably a relic of conventual days, which, after having followed the fashion of each time, has now gradually died out. In 1842 broad Trolly laces of French design and fair workmanship were fabricated in the old cathedral city; where, in the poorer localities near the Bond and the Blossomgate, young women might be seen working their intricate patterns with pillows, bobbins and pins. In 1862 one old woman alone, says our informant, sustains the memory of the craft, her produce a lace of small lozenge-shaped pattern, that earliest of all designs, and a narrow edging known in local parlance by the name of 'fourpenny spot'".[67]

Sample of Ripon lace from the author's collection

In making a comparison of the patterns to other types of Point Ground lace made in England, I visited all the major collections of Point Ground lace and have reached the conclusion that the patterns of Devon Trolly Lace are quite unique. The chart below shows the number of exact matches and similarities from other lace making areas to the Devon Trolly patterns contained in the bag and at the Royal Albert Memorial Museum, Exeter from both the Palliser and Treadwin collections.

Devon Trolly	Downton	Malmesbury	East Midlands	Ripon	Suffolk
Exact matches	2	3	13	2	0
Similarities to	1	1	23	1	2

In total there are 18 exact matches and 25 similarities, accounting for matches and similarities occurring in more than one area. The exact pattern matches are shown:

PG4:   Match-Northampton
         Aylesbury & Luton

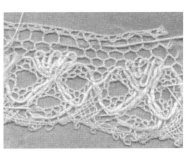

PG10: Match-Aylesbury

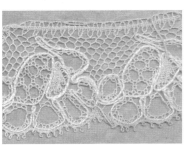

PG33: Match- Northampton

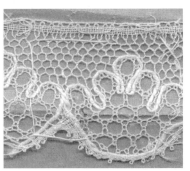

PG34: Match-Northampton

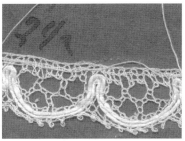

HG1:   Match-Malmesbury
         - different exchange

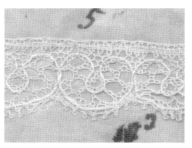

HG2:   Match-Luton

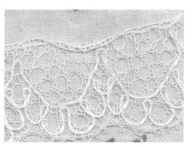

HG4:   Match-Northampton,
         & Downton No.68

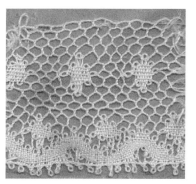

PGNG7: Match-Malmesbury
         has a footside

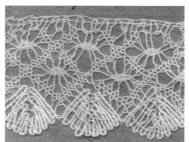

O3: Match-Luton
Museum

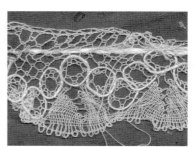

TG5: Match-Malmesbury

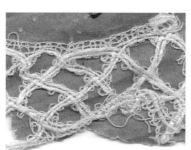

O5: Match-Luton
Book 5-2-3; similar
Museum Book 5-5-1
-Northampton &
Ripon

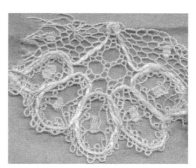

R50: Match – Luton

R38: Match-Northampton

HS5: Match-Northampton

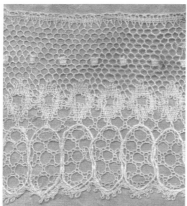

PGT7: Match-
       Northampton &
       Downton

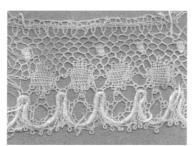

PGT10: Match-
        Northampton

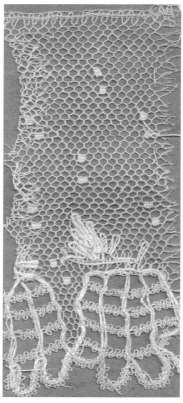

PGT77: Match-
        Northampton
        & MLA

The matches are fairly simple patterns and one wonders whether they were the first patterns to come from France and the Flemish lace making regions to both the Midland and Devon areas and from whence each lace making region developed their individual style; the Midlands area being more 'floral' and the Devon area being more 'geometric'. This is another possible theory to which the answer will never be known, but I am sure that there are further pattern matches to be discovered at some point in the future.

In visiting the various museums, and the Lace Guild HQ at 'The Hollies', I came across one pattern that is known to Devon, Malmesbury, Aylesbury, Northampton, Luton, Tonder, in Denmark and Ipswich, Massachusetts, in the U.S.A.

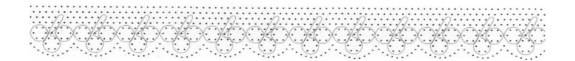

Was this simple pattern one of the first to travel from the Continent to England and Denmark? Did the emigrant lace-makers from England and the Continent take it to New England? I am sure that when further analytical study is undertaken on the Devon Trolly patterns matches will be found with other Continental lace-making areas, but to have a pattern link across three Continents must have some substance – we only have to find out what.

Whilst undertaking my research into Devon Trolly Lace I discovered a Reginald Foster (1595-1681) who was born in Exeter and who emigrated with his wife Judith and his seven children to Ipswich, Massachussetts in 1638 on a vessel embargoed by King Charles! One of his direct descendents, his great great grand-daughter, was Elizabeth Foster Sutton, the lace maker to whom Marta Cotterell Raffell dedicated her book 'The Laces of Ipswich – the art and economics of an early American industry, 1750-1840 '. Is this another link between the Continents? One also wonders whether the 'good wife' Judith was a lace maker herself, perhaps having learned the craft in Devon, or if there are any other, as yet, undiscovered connections.

The decline of the Devonshire Trolly Lace industry

Various relief plans actioned during the first twenty years of the 19th century are documented for the Honiton lace industry and although these actions for relief for the poor lace-makers may have encompassed all those involved in the industry, none of them specifically mention the Trolly Lace being made at the same time. Although the decline had begun in the late 1700s, the "greater part of this occurred in the decade 1810-1820".[68]

There is no doubt that the decline in the need for hand made Trolly Lace was due to the changes in fashion since the Napoleonic Wars and the introduction of lace made by machine. Heathcoat, who moved from Loughborough to Tiverton in Devon, patented his net making machine on March 29th 1809 and went into major production in 1815. This initially gave machine net on which the Honiton sprigs, were attached, rather than joining the sprigs by making hand-made net or brides.

Between 1824 and 1843 Heathcoat patented 14 improvements to his machinery to produce imitation 'French lace'. In 1825 his patent detail describes " Firstly I take a piece of lace and extend it upon the frame. The fabric being thus extended or stretched I trace designs upon it. I then take a sufficient length of purl, and attach it upon the lace, following the design traced thereon. In this manner I form upon the piece of lace bouquets, flowers or other embellishments, in imitation of embroidery".[69] In 1832 he further improved on this labour-intensive method and patented a method of ornamenting embroidering or working devices upon Lace net. "My invention... consists in the employment of certain mechanism, partly resembling that of an ordinary warp lace frame, by which I am enabled to work into the meshes and around the threads of bobbin net lace, and through or upon the fibres comparing other fabrics, stitches or loops of silk, cotton, or other threads for the purpose of producing such fabrics embroidered patterns or devices in strips, zigzags, Grecian borders, scroll work, vandikes and various other running or ornamental form".[70]

Machine-made samples produced by permission of Alison Parker

This continuing improvement in producing imitation Point Ground lace left the lace makers in dire straits and was, in my opinion, the reason that the phrase 'destitute lace makers' was used in the newspaper report of 1841. From the prices quoted in the pattern samples, we can see that the value of the lace had reduced by 52% from 1750 to 1830 and substantiates the claims of those who gave evidence for the 1843 Report on the Employment of Children, e.g. Mr Samuel Evans, draper and lace-dealer of Exmouth said "that the nominal value of the hand-made lace had fallen off at least 60 or 70 per cent "and Susan Crutchell, aged 50 also of Exmouth said "but some years ago when the 'business was more profitable', she used to continue to work all day long, as there was a very ready sale for her kind of work".[71]

The next phase of real interest in Devon lace began with the order from Queen Victoria for her wedding dress, worn in 1840 and made of Honiton Lace. This was closely followed by the introduction of train travel to Exeter, bringing the first organised tourists and the possibility of selling lace to the tourists. The mention of Trolly Lace from this date is negligible as the edict of fashion now dictated a different style and use.

Conclusion

The linen bag that held the Woodbury Salterton lace find had the words 'to burn' written on the outside, in copper plate hand-writing. Was this the instruction of the lace dealer, to avoid having his or her patterns copied by others? Why was the instruction not carried out and the bag stored in the roof of the school for 160 plus years? Why was it put there in the first place and by whom? To these questions we shall never know the answer, but how glad I am that the bag and it's contents are still here, one hundred and sixty years later for all to see, study and re-work.

I do hope that my research has given you, the reader, an insight into this 'lost lace'; I am positive that there is more to discover. The research will continue which will hopefully result in a further publication on the lace-makers of Woodbury Parish, their families and their lives. My 'voyage of discovery' has been energising, in that the more I discovered the more I wished to delve and it has brought to the surface my love of social history, that has probably been suppressed and ignored since my schooldays.

REFERENCES

1. Penderel Moody, 1909, p1
2. Mary Sharpe, 1913, p167
3. N. Hudson Moore, 1905, p105
4. Palliser, 1865, 1st Edition, p387
5. Ibid, 1869, 2nd Edition, p360
6. Ibid, 1902 4th Edition, p413
7. Yallop, 1992, p80
8. N. Hudson Moore, p190
9. Neville Jackson, 1900, p146
10. Penderel Moody, 1907, p21
11. Bullock, 1981, p17
12. Caulfield & Saward, 1882 p501
13. Ibid,
14. Wright, 1919, p212
15. Ibid, p64
16. Chope, 1918, p136
17. Pamela Sharpe, 2002, p105
18. Palliser, 4th Edition, p413
19. Ibid,
20. Levey, 1983, p58
21. Eirwen Jones, p161
22. Palliser, 1st Edition, p387
23. Ibid, 4th Edition, p414
24. Ibid
25. House of Commons, 1843, p27
26. Ibid, p28
27. Ibid, p28
28. Ibid, p29
29. Jourdain, 1905, p95
30. House of Commons, 1843, p33
31. Eirwen Jones, p161
32. Yallop, 1992, p80
33. White's Directory, 1850
34. Head, 1921, p91
35. Harrison, 1984, p55
36. Palliser, 1st Edition, p387
37. Ibid,
38. Levey, 1983, p124
39. Ibid, p57
40. Report of Juries 1852, p1013
41. Bath & West Agricultural Society Report 1876
42. Penderel Moody, 1907, p21
43. Wright, 1919, p126
44. Ibid, p125
45. Palliser, 1st Edition, p270
46. Yallop, 1992, p155
47. Clifford, 1981, p46
48. Lowes, 1908, p162
49. Jourdain, 1905, p96
50. Winser, 1913, p38
51. Levey, 1983, p58
52. Ibid,
53. Ibid,
54. Palliser, 1st Edition, p387
55. Ibid, p74
56. Sydney, Vol1., p111
57. Ibid,
58. D.R.O. Q.S. Box 370
59. Palliser, 1st Edition, p406
60. House of Commons, 1843, p32
61. English Women's Domestic magazine, Vol.1 1866, p59-60
62. Penderel Moody, 1907, p23
63. Ibid,
64. Bigg-Wither, 1936, p35
65. Penderel Moody, p24
66. Earnshaw, 1982, p173
67. Palliser, 4th Edition, p371
68. Yallop, 1982, p 92
69. DRO, Heathcoat Patents no. 5103
70. Ibid, no. 6222
71. House of Commons, 1843, pp31-32

BIBLIOGRAPHY

Baring Gould, S., *The Book of Devon* (3rd edition) 1909

Bigg-Wither, Ruth, *Cameos from a Lace Cupbaord* (National Libraries) 1936

Bouvet, Claudette & Michel., *Norman Laces – Blonde Lace of Caen*

Bullock, Alice-May, *Lace and Lacemaking,* (Batsford) 1981

Caulfield, S.F.A.& Saward, B.C., *The Dictionary of Needlework* (2nd Edition) 1885

Chope, R.Pearse, *Early Tours in Devon & Cornwall* 1918 (rep. David & Charles) 1967

Clifford, C.R., *The Lace Dictionary* (Gale Research Co.) 1981

Eirwen Jones, Mary, *The Romance of Lace* (Staple Press, London/NY) 1951

Earnshaw, Pat., *A Dictionary of Lace* (Shire Publications) 1982

Harrison, E. Michael, *Otterton – A Devon Village* 1984

Head, Mrs., *The Lace and Embroidery Collector-*
                 A Guide to Old Lace & Embroidery (Jenkins) 1921

House of Commons, *2nd Report on the Commission for enquiry into the employment of*
                 children in mines & manufactures. 1843

Hudson-Moore, N., *The Lace Book* (Chapman & Hall, London) 1905

Huetson, T.L., *Lace & Bobbins* (David & Charles) 1973

Inder, P., *Honiton Lace* (Exeter Museum) 1971

Jones, Mary Eirwen, *The Romance of Lace* (Staple Press) 1951

Jourdain, M., *Old Lace – A Handbook for Collectors* (Batsford) 1905

Levey, Santina, *Lace – A History* (Victoria & Albert Museum) 1983

Lowes, Mrs., *Chats on Old Lace and Needlework* (Unwin) 1908

Lysons, Rev. Daniel, *Magna Britannica- Great Britain-Vol 6.,* 1822

Moody, Miss A. Penderel, *Devon Pillow Lace* 1907

Moody, Miss A. Penderel, *Lace Making and Collecting* 1909

Nevill Jackson, Mrs F., *Old Hand Made Lace with a Dictionary of Lace*
                            (Dover Publications Reprint) 1981

Palliser, Mrs Bury, *The History of Lace* 1st Edition, 1865, 2nd , 1869, 4th , 1902

Reigate, Emily, *An Illustrated Guide to Lace* (Antique Collector's Club) 1986

Sharpe, Mary, *Point & Pillow Lace* (John Murray) 1913

Sharpe, Pamela, *Population and Society in an East Devon Parish –*
                 Reproducing Colyton 1540-1840 (Exeter Uni. Press) 2002

Sydney, William C., *England & the English in the 18th Century* 1891

Thornton, Revd. W.H., *Devonshire Associations – Vol 39* 1907

Van der Meulen-Nulle, L.W., *Lace* (Merlin Press) 1963

Winser, Margaret & Aileen, *An Elementary Course of Practical Lace-Making*
                         (E.J. Arnold & Son,) 1913

Wright, Thomas, *Romance to the Lace Pillow 1919,* (Ruth Bean) 1982

Yallop, John, *The History of the Honiton Lace Industry* (Exeter Uni. Press) 1992

ARTICLES, DIRECTORIES, NEWSPAPERS & PERIODICALS
Bath & West Catalogues

Cassell's Family Magazine, December 1893

Devon Record Office, Quarter Sessions

English Women's Domestic Magazine, 1866

Exeter Flying Post

The Boston Gazette & County Journal, 1774

Weldon's Practical Needlework, No 229, Vol 3

White's Directory 1850

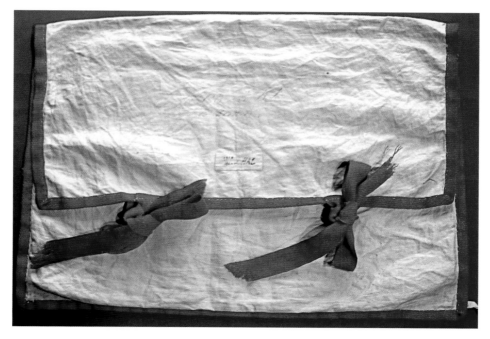

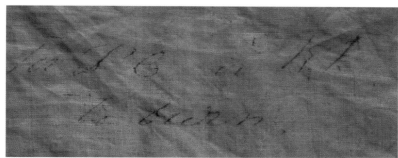

The Lace Dealer's Bag

Queen Victoria's work-bag

39

The sachet

The Sampler for Queen Victoria

A page of Devon Trolly Lace samples

The only piece of black lace in the bag

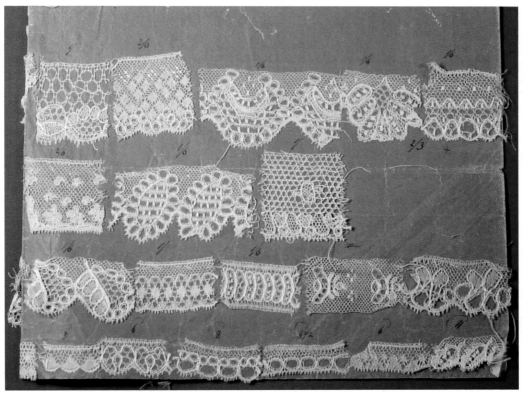

A half page of Devon Trolly lace samples

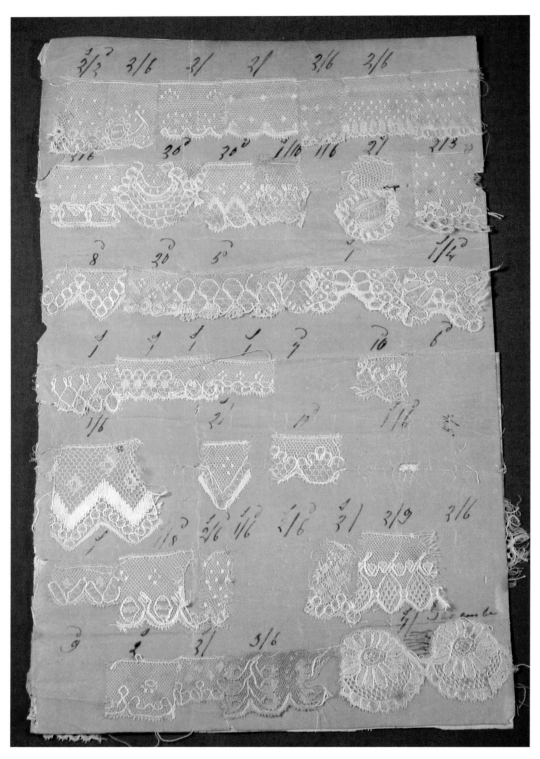

An even bigger selection to choose from!

Amelia Margareta Dixon
(1756-1841)
produced by kind permission of
Enrico Paoletti and Bonhams Associates

Trolly Bobbins highly decorated dated 1696, 1700

Old and modern trolly bobbins in use

The Devon Trolly Patterns

One of the crucial decisions to make when re-drawing old lace patterns is whether to rework them as they were produced or as the modern lace maker would now wish them to be. Following discussions with lace colleagues the consensus was for the patterns to be re-drawn as a 'trued up' version. The next decision was whether they would be worked by today's methods or by those of earlier times: again it was decided to re-work them as they would have been worked unless there was an improvement in the method that would improve the appearance of the lace for today's discerning lace maker.

The lace patterns have been re-drawn using the Lace 2000 computer programme. They ranged in angle from 45 to 60 degrees and have been re-drawn as near to their original angle as the computer programme would permit. The prickings however, are true to the original pattern designs. The prickings have been retained as edgings, their original format, but the possibility of forming corners and motifs is a challenge.

The lace makers who attended the OIDFA 2002 Congress showed a keen interest in the lace find and the most frequently asked question was "When are the patterns going to be available"? I do hope that this first book of Devon Trolly lace encourages all lace makers to attempt some of these lost patterns and, that when working them you experience the same anticipation and excitement, felt by Caroline, Liz and myself in October 2002 when the first three samples were produced.

The patterns in the bag were categorised in the following way:

I	1-16	Insertion patterns
HS	1-10	contained Half Stitch blocks
HG	1-11	Honeycombe ground
TGV	1-18	Torchon ground variation
KG	1-31	Kat Sticth ground
O	1-32	Odd patterns that do not fit in any other category
PGNG	1-27	Point ground with no gimp
PG	1-77	Point ground with a gimp
PGT	1-107	Point ground with gimp and tallies
M	1-6	Metallic laces
R	1-61	Patterns on the Royal sampler (those included have duplicates in the bag).

For each section the patterns are then catalogued in width order.

When the number of gimp threads are given for each pattern, 'S' represents a single gimp and Pr means a pair of gimp threads.

The price is given as on the pattern sheets. The equivalent price today, from 1750 and 1830, is also given for comparison and disbelief!

Blow Brain

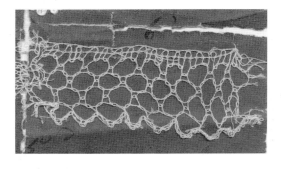

Bobbins   8 Pairs

Thread   120/2 Cotton

Cost per yard	6d
1750	£2-63
1830	£1-35

Method:

Hang 2 prs on the top 4 pin holes.

Twist each pr 3 times

W.S. to enclose the pin and twist 3 times. Work vertically down the columns.

Work W.S. and 3 twists throughout.

Sometimes a square leadwork (a spat) was made in the middle row.

Pattern   PG7

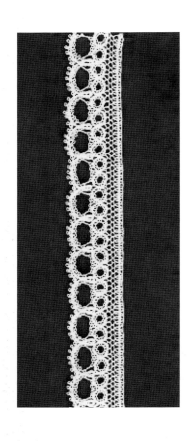

Bobbins	14 pairs
Thread	120/2 Cotton
Gimp	Perle 12 1 S + 1 Pr
Cost per yard	3 ½ d
1750	£1-54
1830	77p

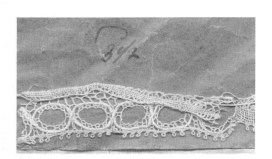

Pattern PG9

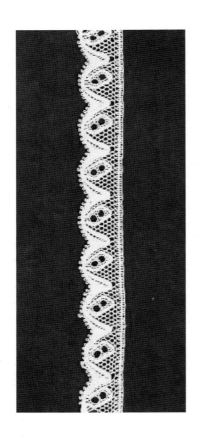

Bobbins	15 pairs
Thread	120/2 Cotton
Gimp	Perle 8 2 S
Cost per yard	6 d
1750	£2-63
1830	£1-35

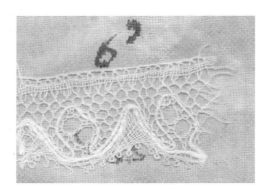

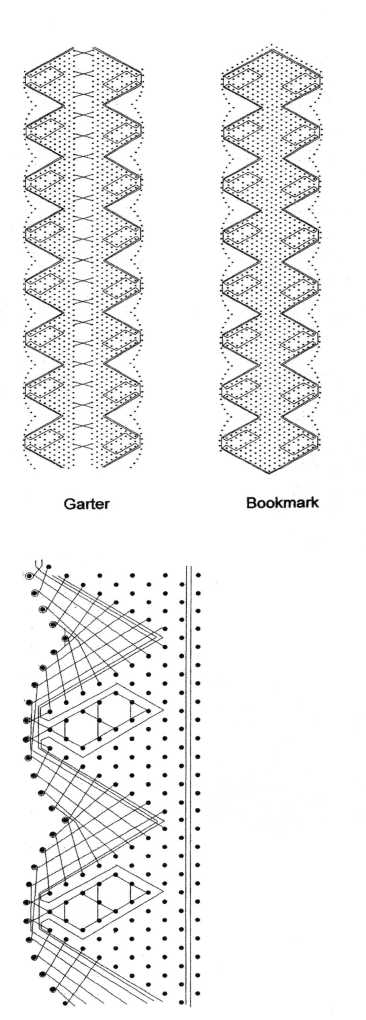

Garter

Bookmark

Pattern PG10

Bobbins	15 pairs
Thread	120/2 Cotton
Gimp	Cotton a Broder 16 1 Pr
Cost per yard	8 d
1750	£3-51
1830	£1-80

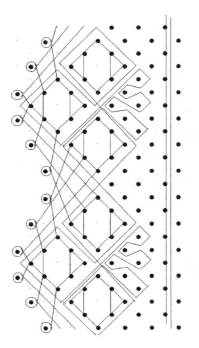

57

Pattern   PGT2

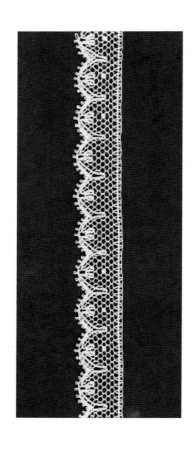

Bobbins   15 pairs

Thread   120/2 Cotton

Gimp   Perle 12
1 S

Cost per yard   6 d

1750   £2-63

1830   £1-35

Pattern PG16

Bobbins	15 pairs
Thread	120/2 Cotton
Gimp	Perle 12 2 S

Cost per yard	5 d
1750	£2-19
1830	£1-26

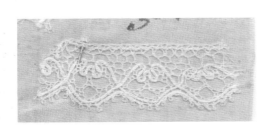

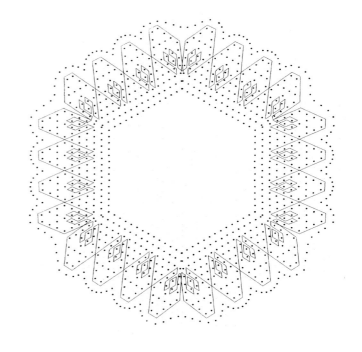

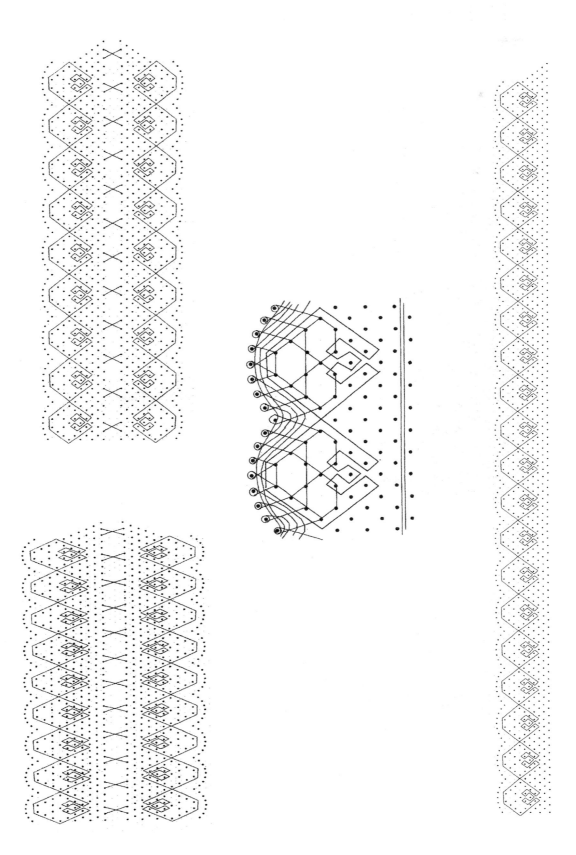

Pattern   PG19

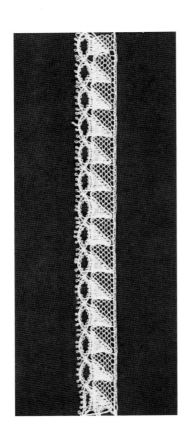

Bobbins	15 pairs
Thread	120/2 Cotton
Gimp	Perle 12 3 S
Cost per yard	5 d
1750	£2-19
1830	£1-26

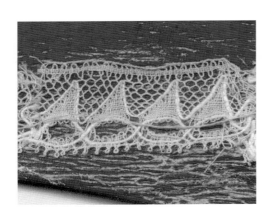

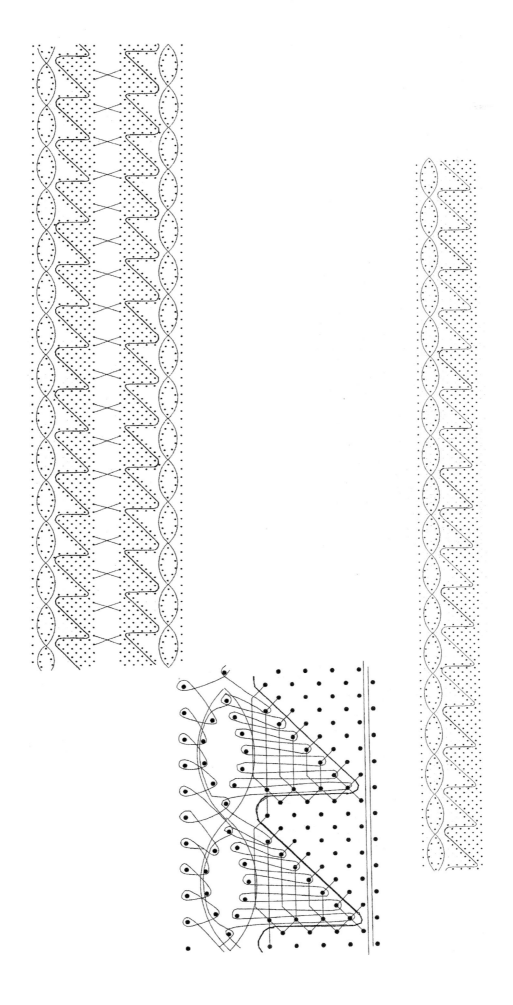

Pattern   PGNG6

Bobbins	18 pairs
Thread	120/2 Cotton
Cost per yard	1/2d
1750	£6-13
1830	£3-15

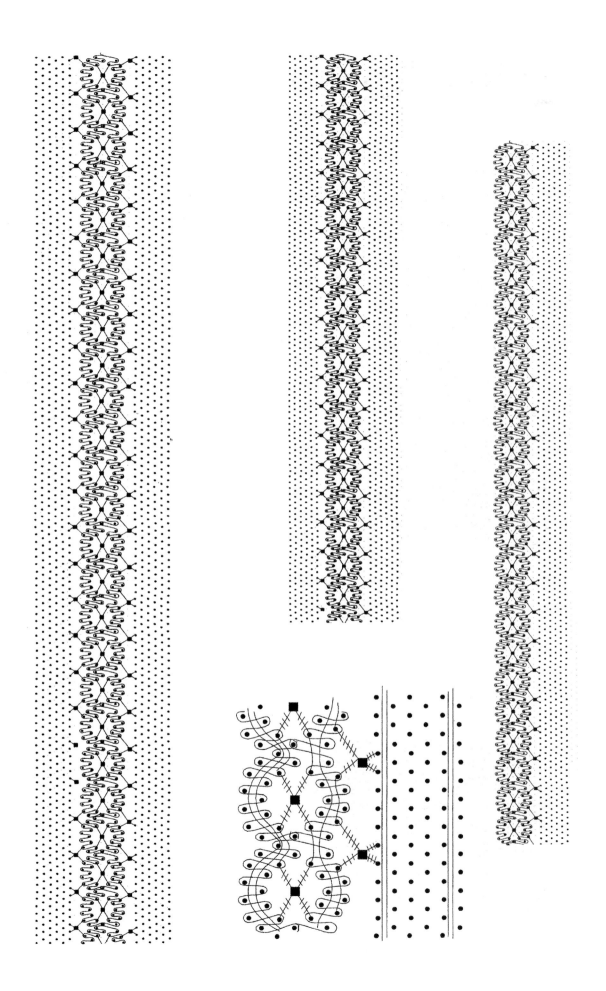

Pattern TGV1

Bobbins   12 pairs

Thread   120/2 Cotton

Gimp   Perle 12
        2 S

Cost per yard   4 d

1750   £1-75

1830   90p

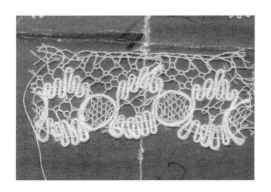

Pattern HG3

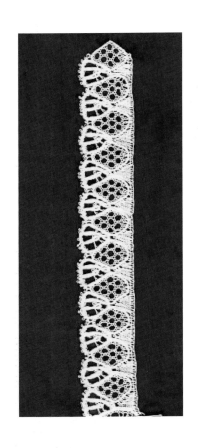

Bobbins	12 pairs
Thread	120/2 Cotton
Gimp	Perle 8 2 S
Cost per yard	6 d
1750	£2-63
1830	£1-35

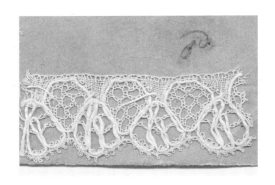

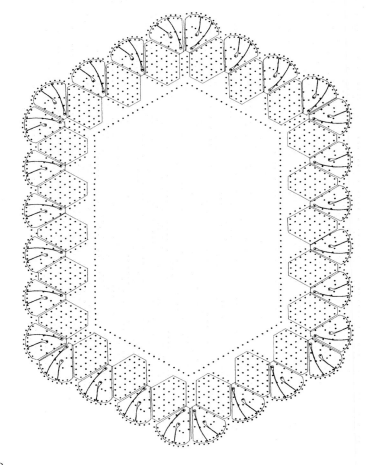

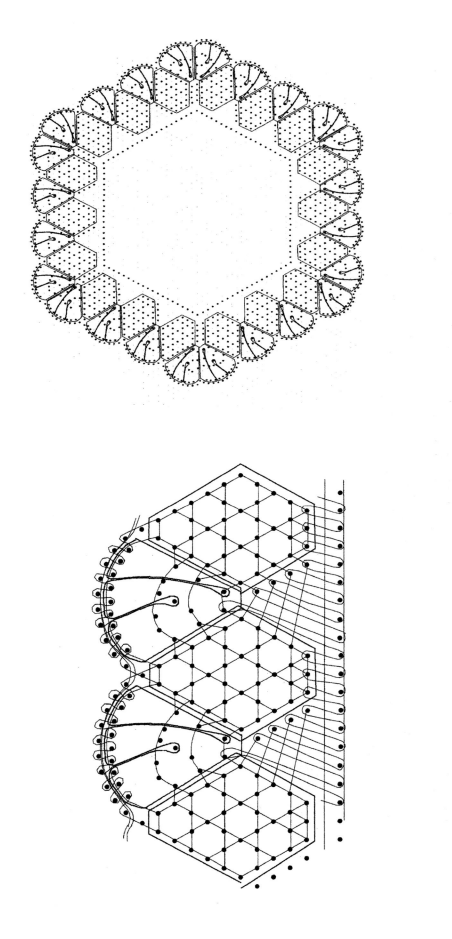

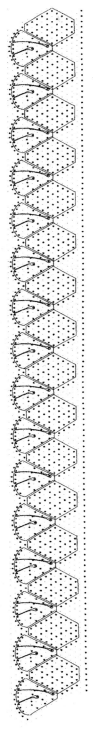

Pattern   PG33

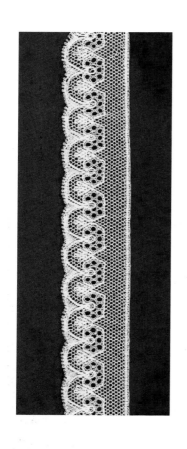

Bobbins	24 pairs
Thread	120/2 Cotton
Gimp	Perle 12
	3 S

Cost per yard	1/2d
1750	£6-13
1830	£3-15

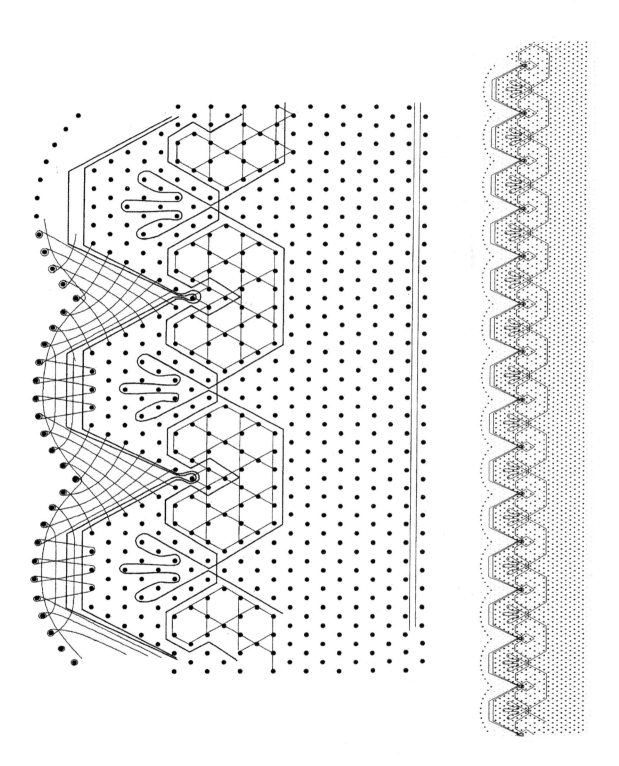

Pattern   I6

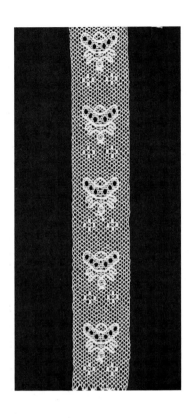

Bobbins   25 pairs

Thread   120/2 Cotton

Gimp   Perle 12
1Pr

Cost per yard   ?

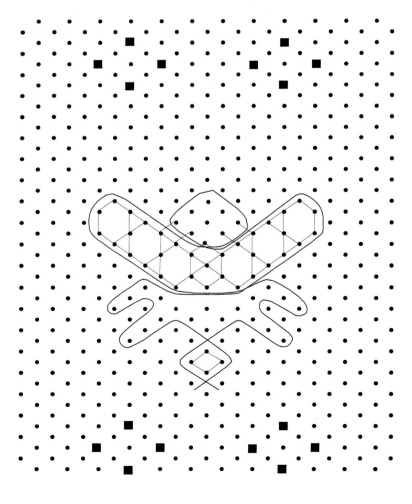

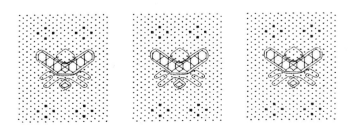

Pattern   PG36

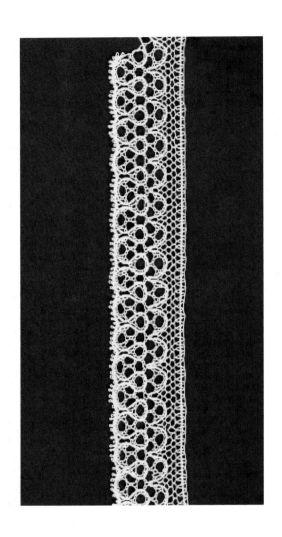

Bobbins	20 pairs
Thread	120/2 Cotton
Gimp	Perle 12
	2 S

Cost per yard	7 d
1750	£3-06
1830	£1-57

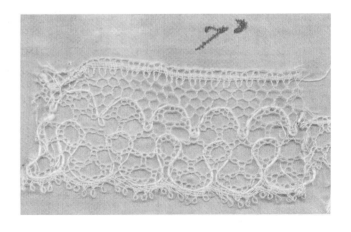

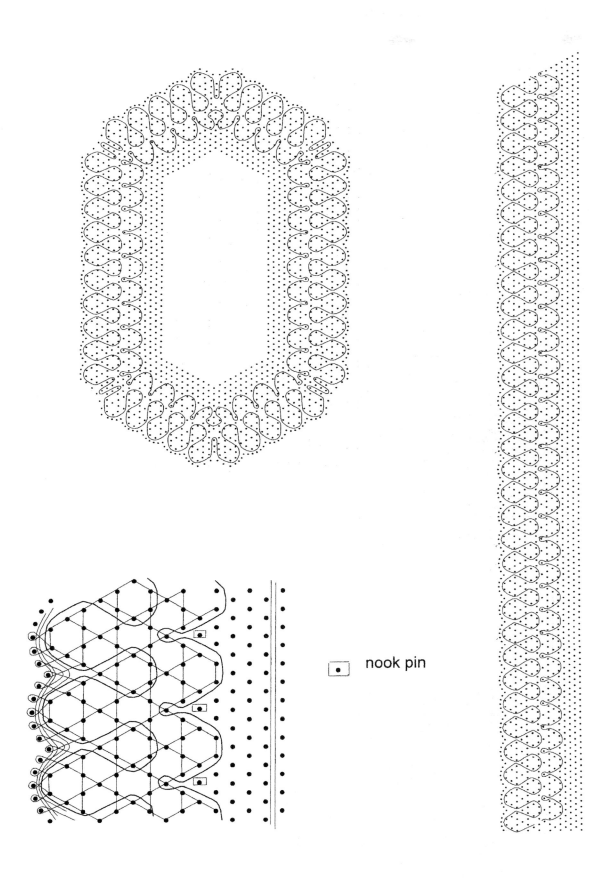

nook pin

Pattern   PG37

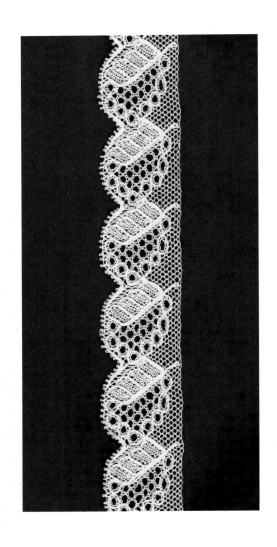

Bobbins	24 pairs
Thread	120/2 Cotton
Gimp	Perle 12 2 Pr
Cost per yard	1/6 d
1750	£7-88
1830	£4-05

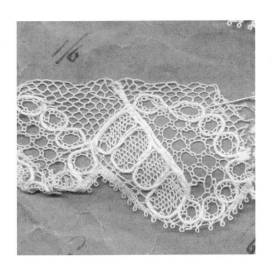

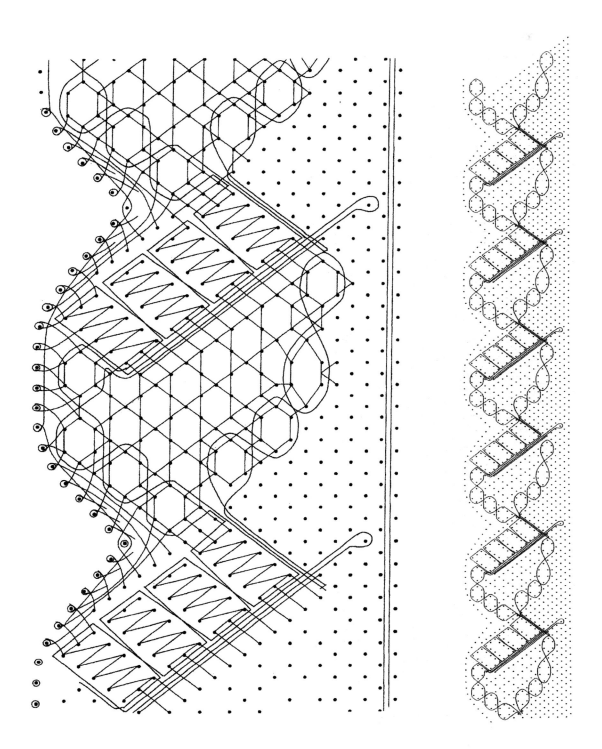

Pattern   PG39

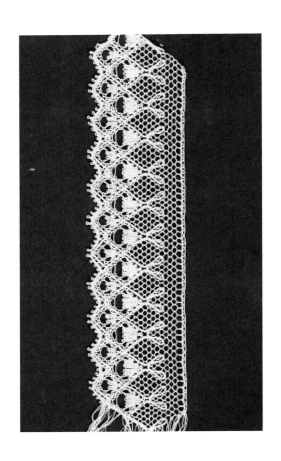

Bobbins	27 pairs
Thread	120/2 Cotton
Gimp	Perle 12 1 S + 1 Pr
Cost per yard	1/-
1750	£5-25
1830	£2-70

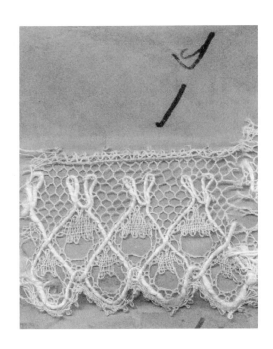

Pattern PG40

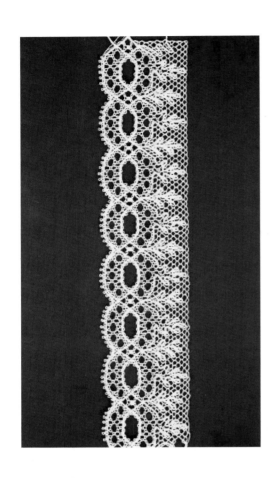

Bobbins	25 pairs
Thread	120/2 Cotton
Gimp	Perle 12 2 Pr
Cost per yard	1/-
1750	£5-25
1830	£2-70

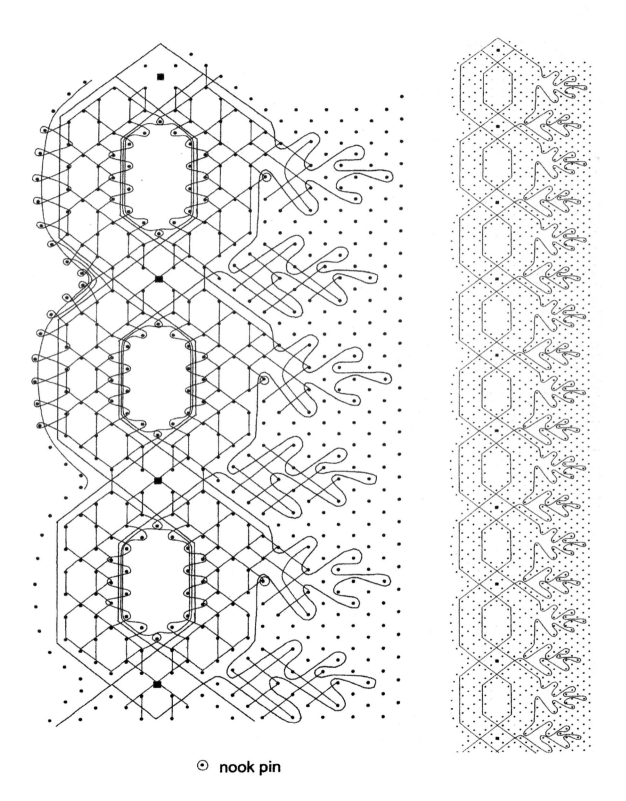

⊙ nook pin

Pattern   PG41

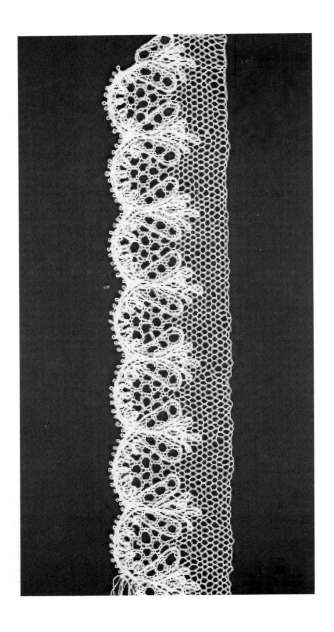

Bobbins   25 pairs

Thread   120/2 Cotton

Gimp   Perle 12
1 Pr

Cost per yard   ?

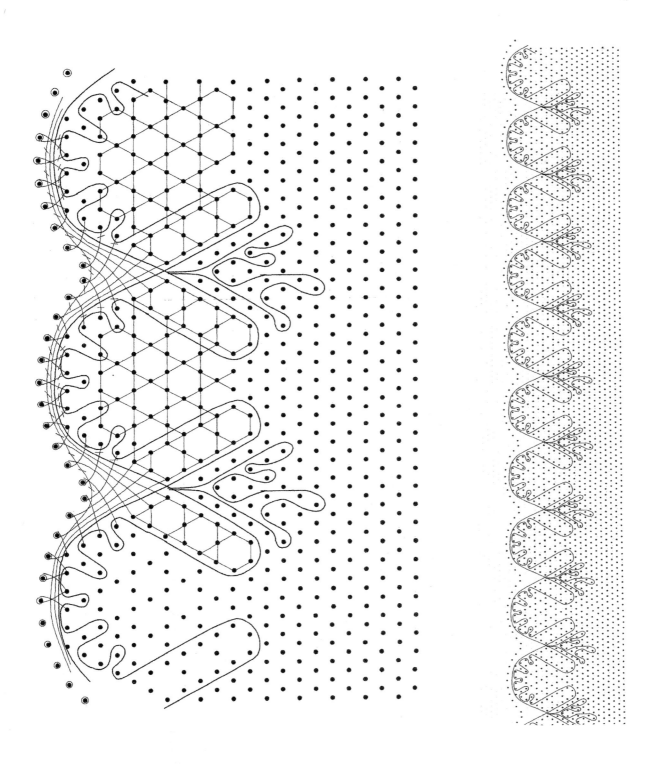

Pattern I9

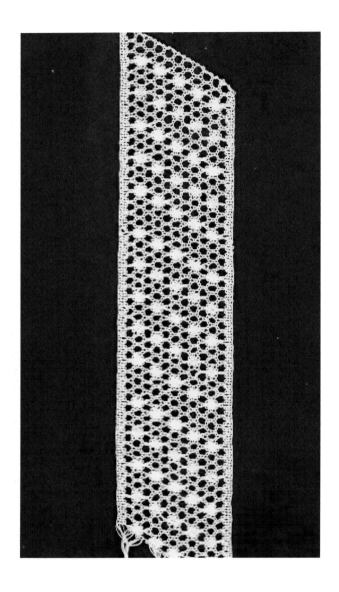

Bobbins   28 pairs

Thread   Tanne 80

Cost per yard   1/-

1750   £5-25

1830   £2-70

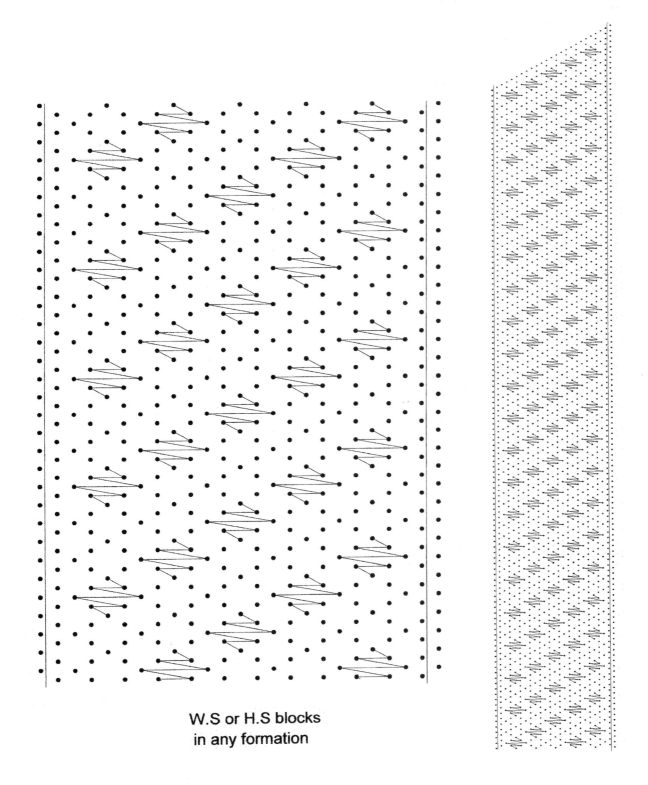

W.S or H.S blocks
in any formation

85

Pattern   TGV7

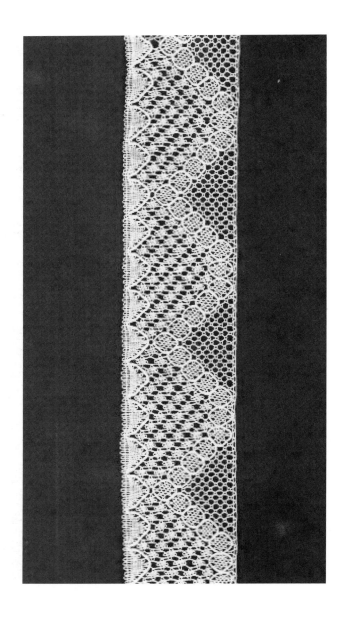

Bobbins	27 pairs
Thread	120/2 Cotton
Gimp	Coton a Broder 25 1 S + 1 Pr
Cost per yard	1/-
1750	£5-25
1830	£2-70

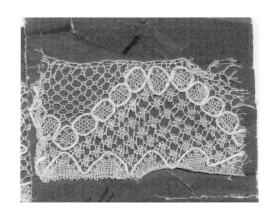

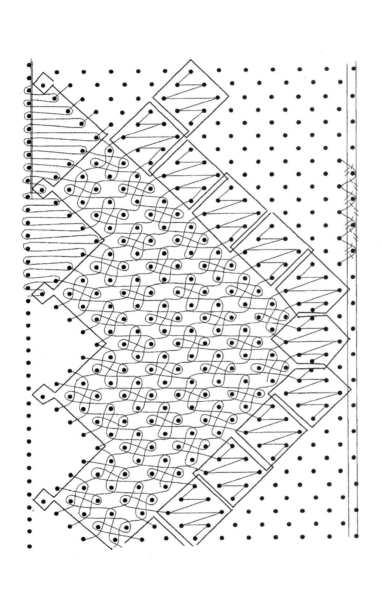

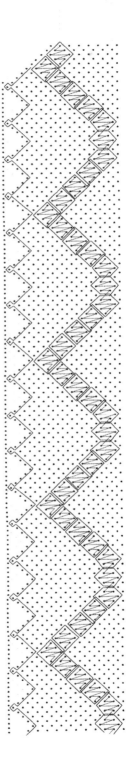

Pattern O12

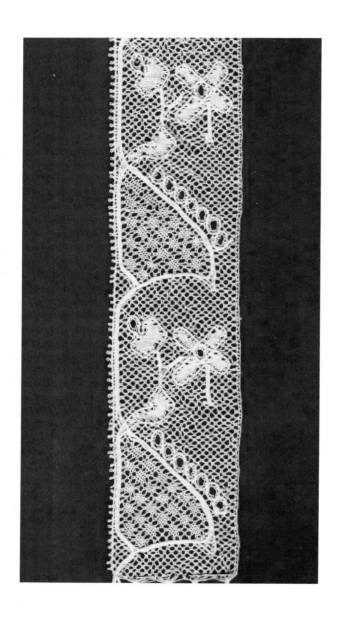

Bobbins	38 pairs
Thread	120/2 Cotton
Gimp	Perle 12 4 S + 3 Prs
Cost per yard	2/2d
1750	£11-38
1830	£5-84

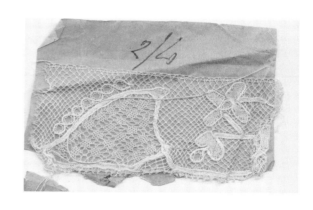

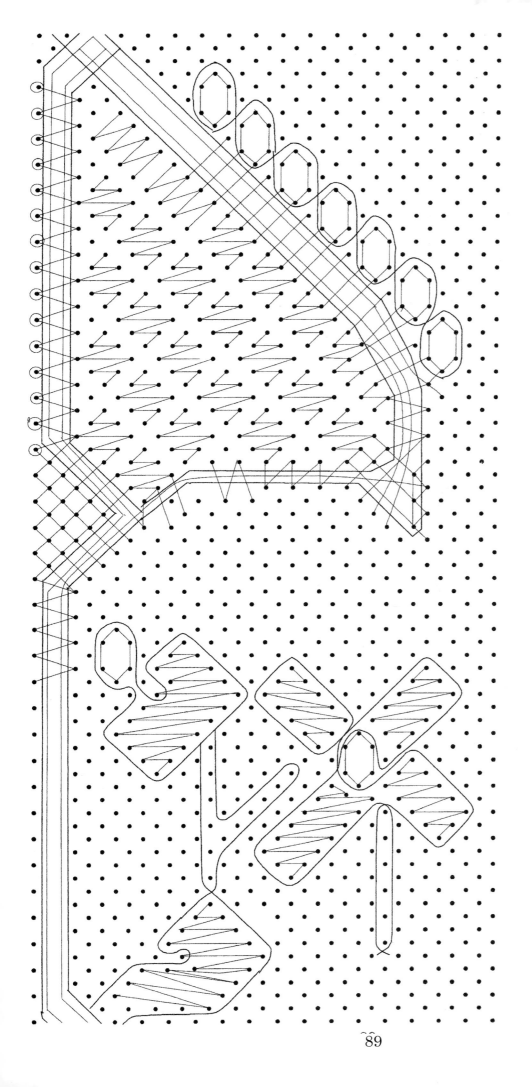
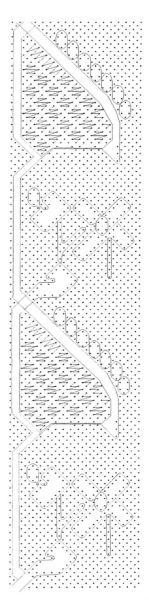

Pattern HS3

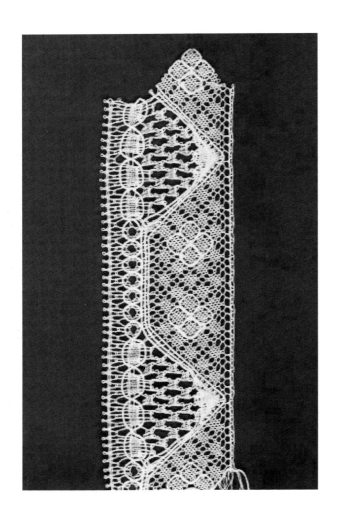

Bobbins   31 pairs

Thread   120/2 Cotton

Gimp   Perle 12
2 S

Cost per yard	21d
1750	£9-20
1830	£4-72

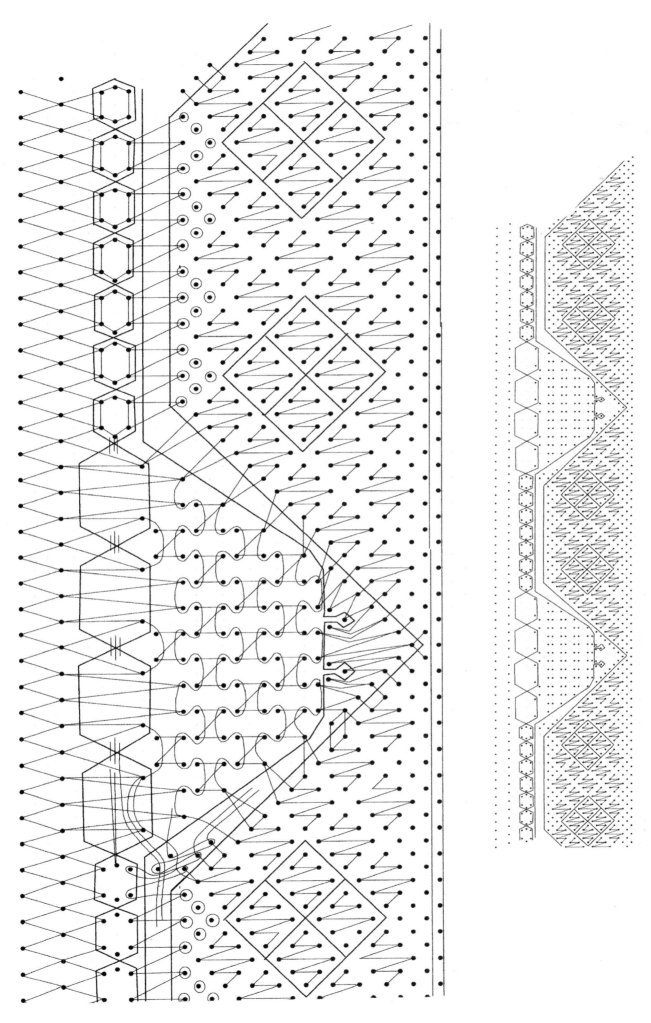

Pattern   PG55

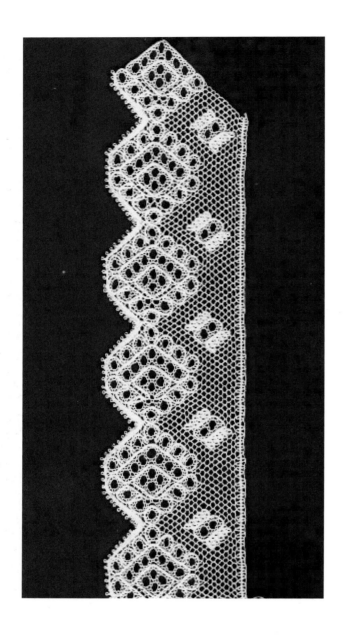

Bobbins   37 pairs

Thread   120/2 Cotton

Gimp   Coton a
Broder 25
2 Prs

Cost per yard   2/-

1750   £10-50

1830   £5-40

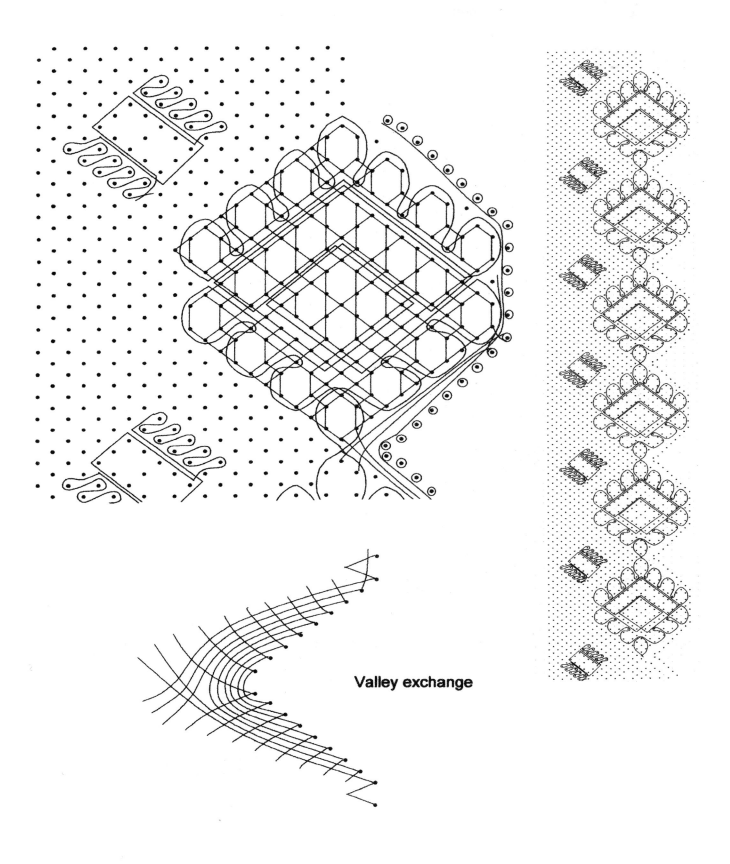

Valley exchange

Pattern   PGT46

Bobbins	40 pairs
Thread	120/2 Cotton
Gimp	Coton a Broder 25 3 Prs

Cost per yard	2/6d
1750	£13-13
1830	£6-75

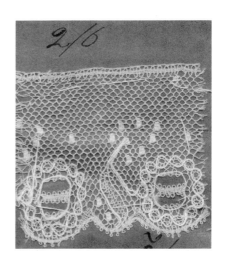

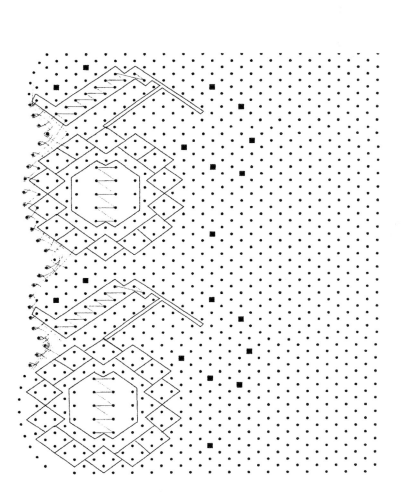

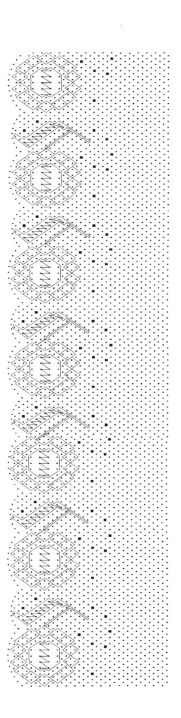

Pattern   PGT48

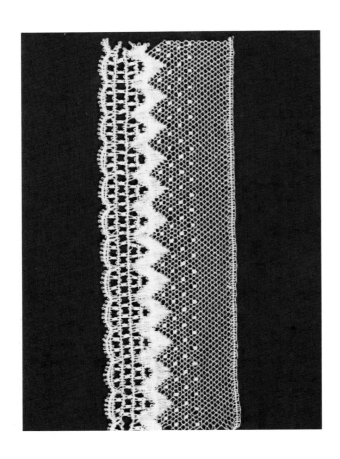

Bobbins	pairs
Thread	120/2 Cotton
Gimp	Coton a Broder 30 1 S
Cost per yard	2/9d
1750	£14-45
1830	£7-42

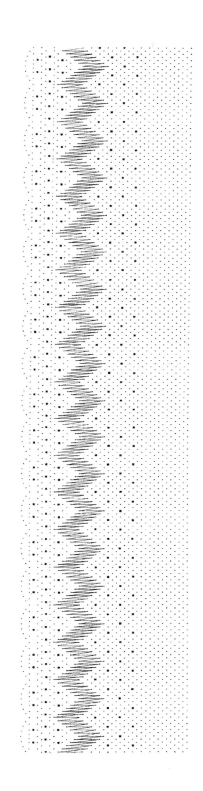

Pattern   PGNG21

Bobbins	42 pairs
Thread	Unity 150

Cost per yard	1/6d
1750	£7-88
1830	£4-05

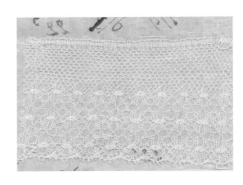

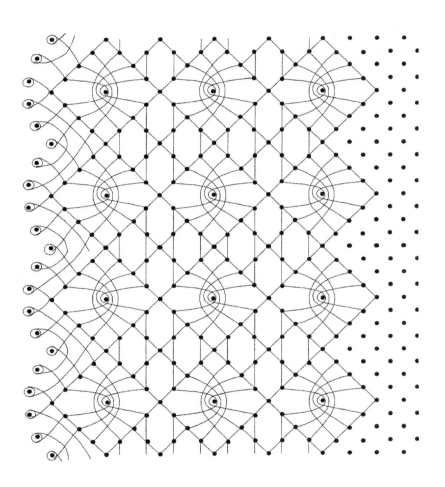

Pattern   HS6

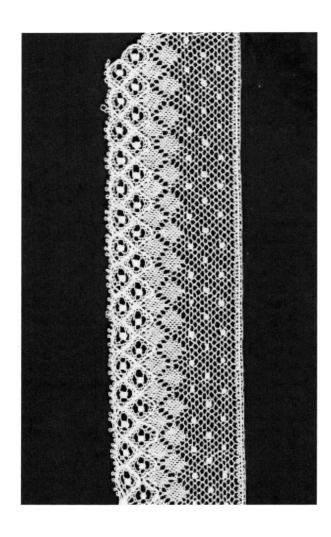

Bobbins	37 pairs
Thread	120/2 Cotton
Gimp	Perle 12 2 Pr

Cost per yard	2/-
1750	£10-50
1830	£5-40

100

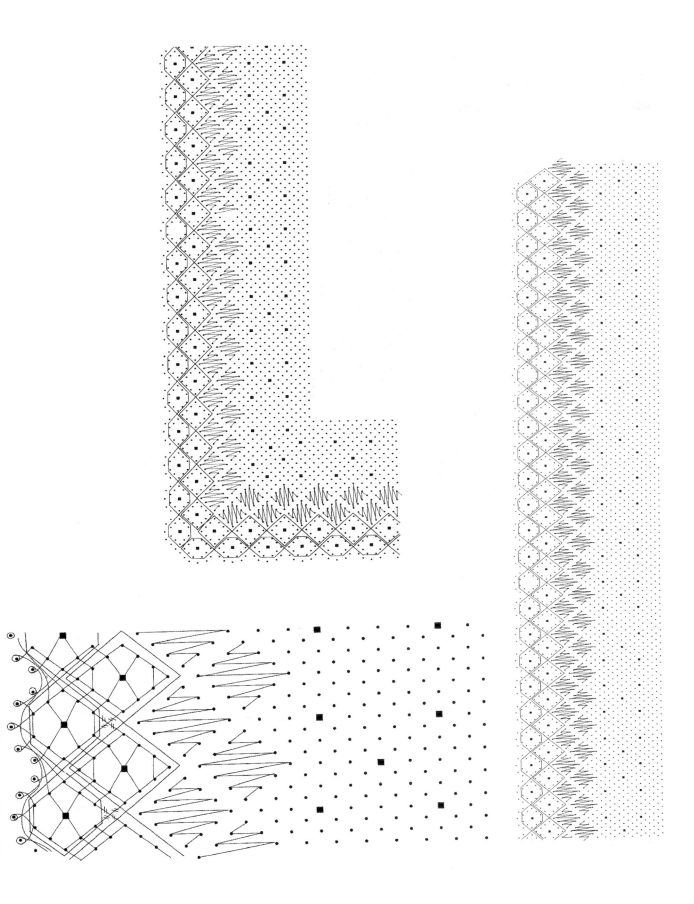

Pattern   PGT62

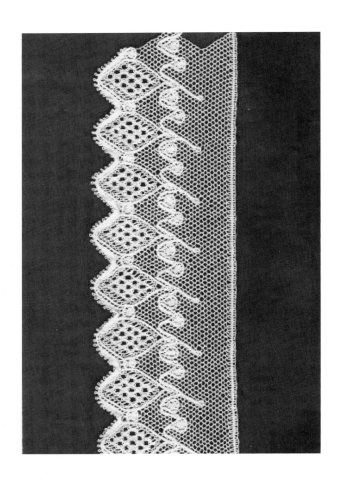

Bobbins   44 pairs

Thread   120/2 Cotton

Gimp

Cost per yard   2/9d

1750   £14-45

1830   £7-42

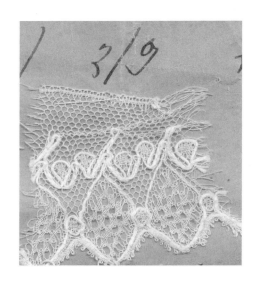

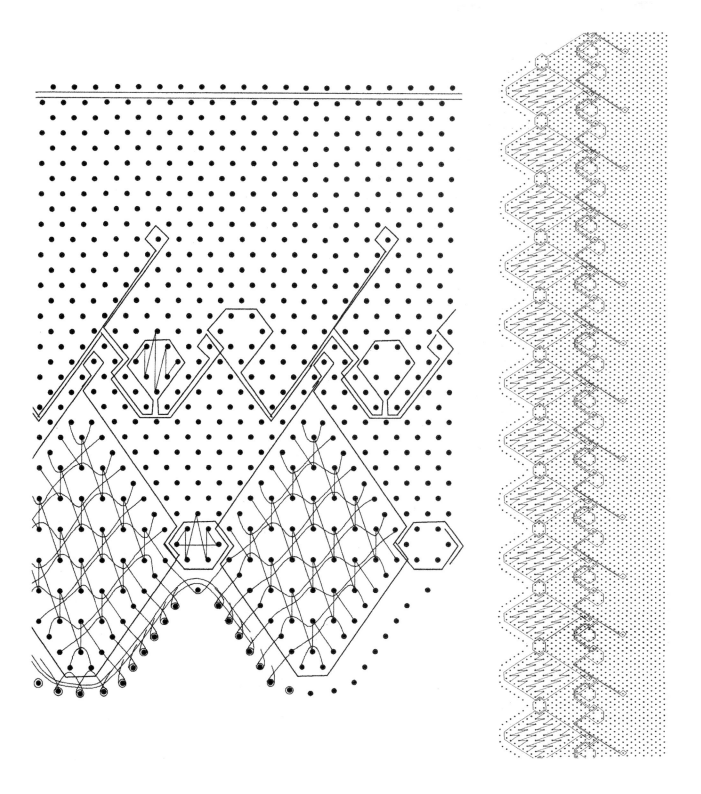

Pattern   PGT63

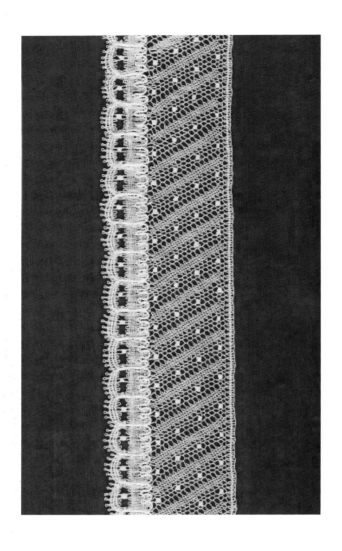

Bobbins	34 pairs
Thread	120/2 Cotton
Gimp	Coton a Broder 16 1Pr
Cost per yard	1/8d
1750	£8-76
1830	£4-50

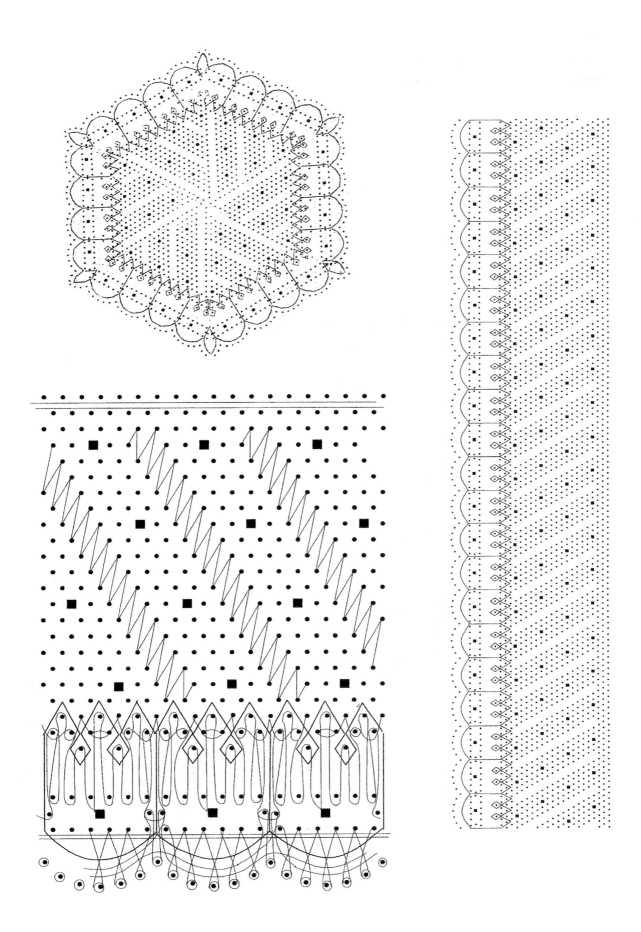

Pattern   PGT68

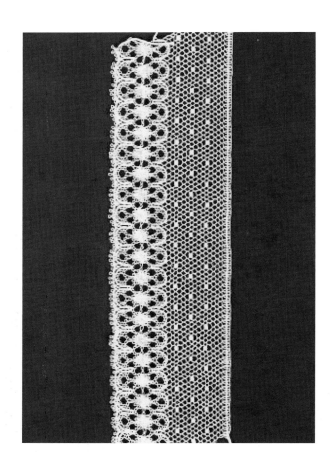

Bobbins	35 pairs
Thread	120/2 Cotton
Gimp	Perle 12 2 S
Cost per yard	1/6d
1750	£7-88
1830	£4-05

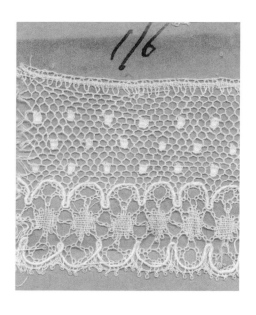

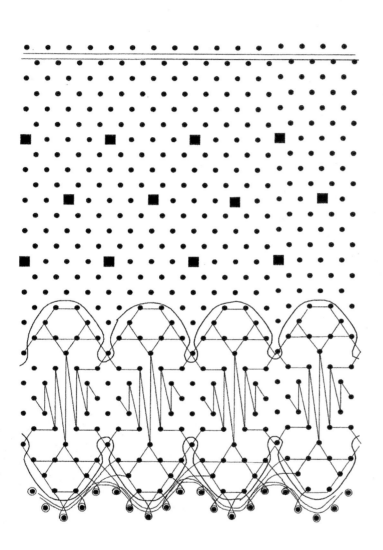

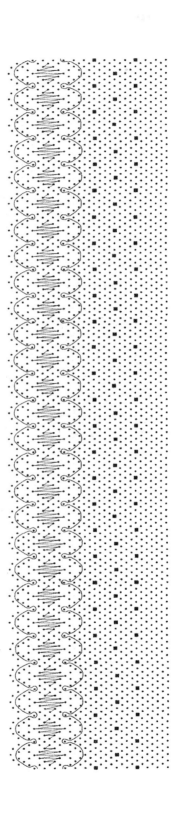

Pattern   PGT81

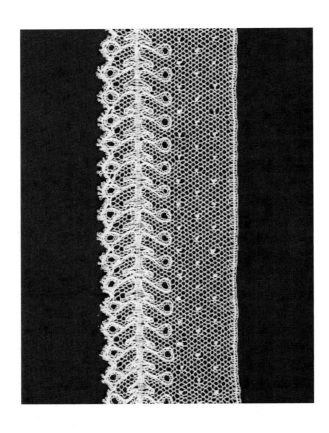

Bobbins	42 pairs
Thread	120/2 Cotton
Gimp	Perle 12
Cost per yard	1/6d
1750	£7-88
1830	£4-05

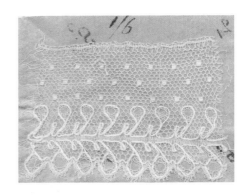

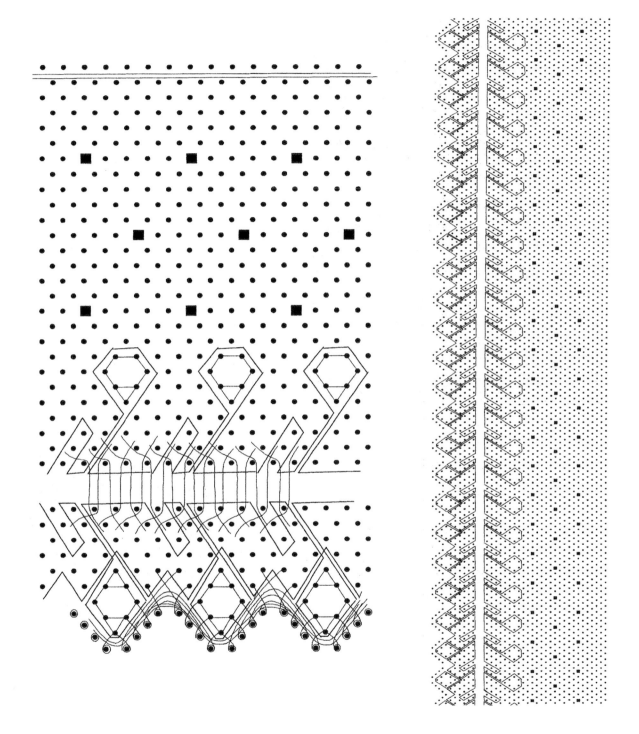

Pattern   PGT87

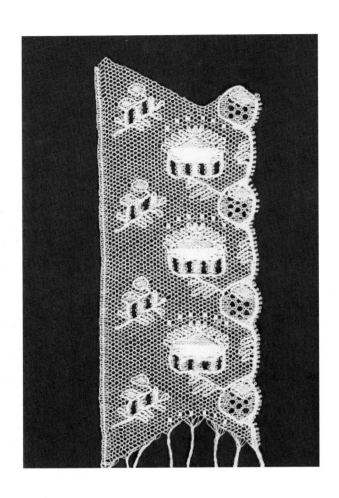

Bobbins   49 pairs

Thread   120/2 Cotton

Gimp   Coton a
Broder 20
2S +1 Pr

Cost per yard   ?

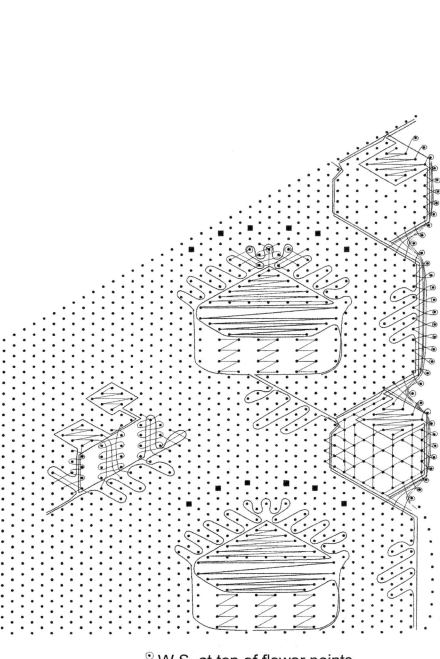

⊙ W.S. at top of flower points

Gimp weaver

Pattern   PGT90

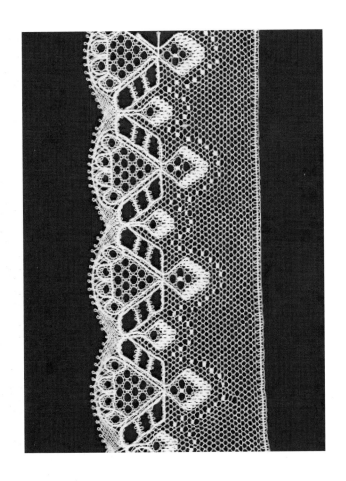

Bobbins	49 pairs
Thread	120/2 Cotton
Gimp	Perle 12 3 S
Cost per yard	2/-
1750	£10-50
1830	£5-40

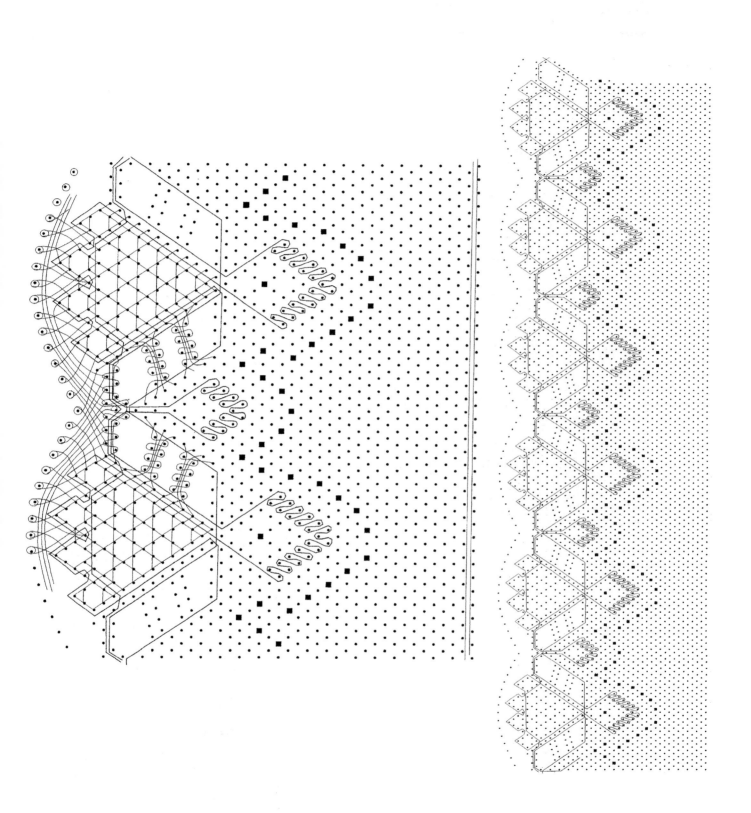

Pattern   PGT91

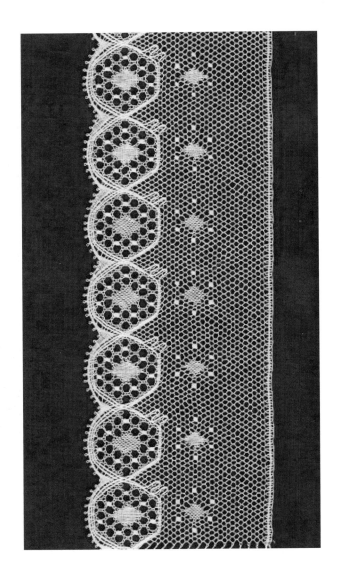

Bobbins	48 pairs
Thread	120/2 Cotton
Gimp	Perle 12 2 Pr

Cost per yard	1/8d
1750	£8-76
1830	£4-50

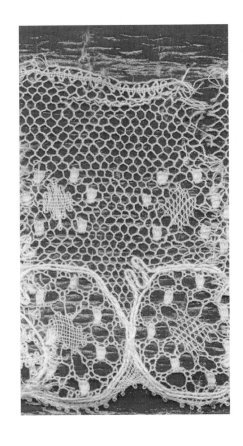

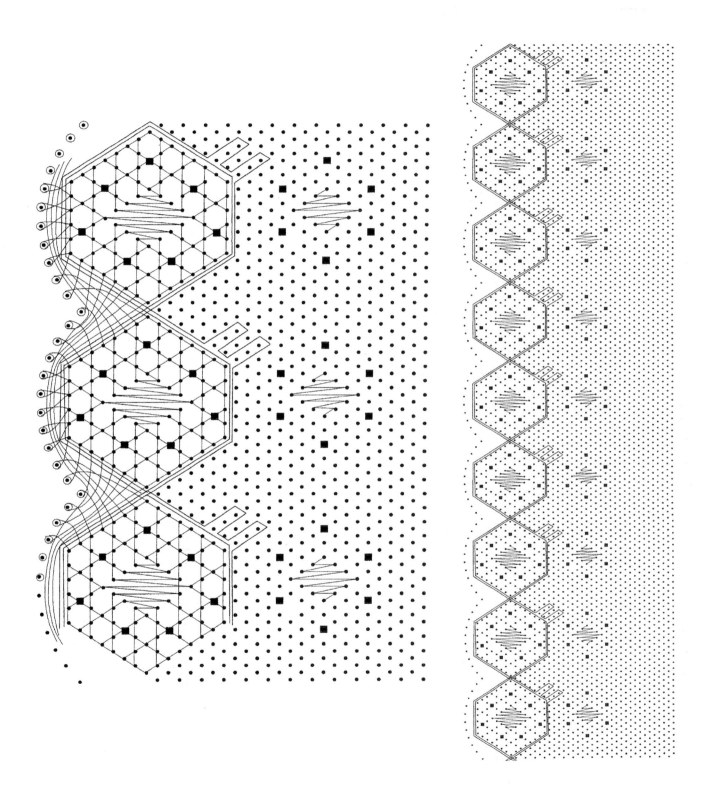

Pattern   I14

Bobbins   58 pairs

Thread   120/2 Cotton

Gimp   Coton a
Broder 16
2 Pr

Cost per yard   5/-

1750   £26-27

1830   £13-30

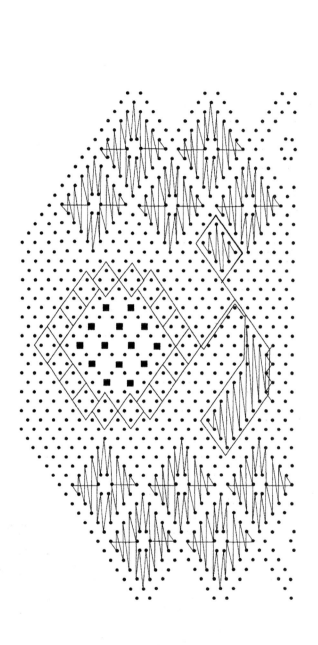

Pattern R19

Bobbins   68 pairs

Thread   120/2 Cotton

Gimp   Coton a
Broder 25
3 Pr

Cost per yard   ?

Pattern   TGV16

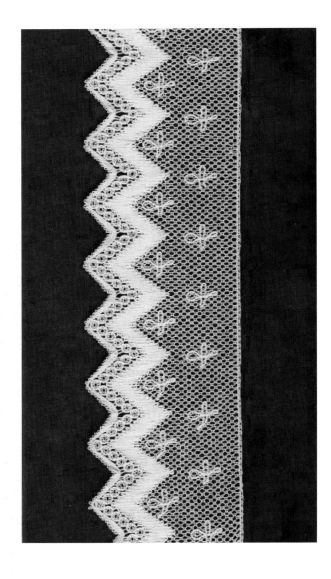

Bobbins   44 pairs

Thread   120/2 Cotton

Gimp   Coton a
              Broder 12
              1 S +2 Pr

Cost per yard   2/-

1750   £10-50

1830   £5-40

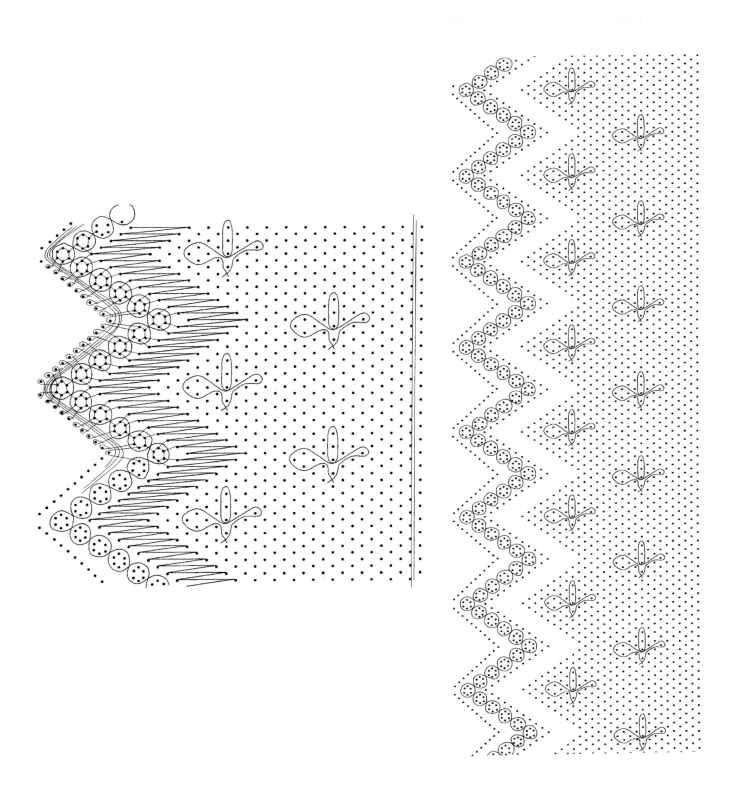

Pattern   PGT96

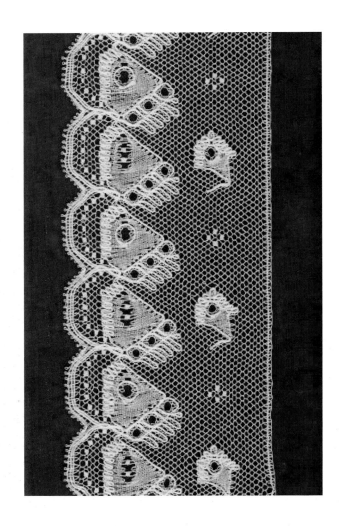

Bobbins	51 pairs
Thread	120/2 Cotton
Gimp	Coton a Broder 16 2 S +1 Pr

Cost per yard	3/-
1750	£15-76
1830	£7-98

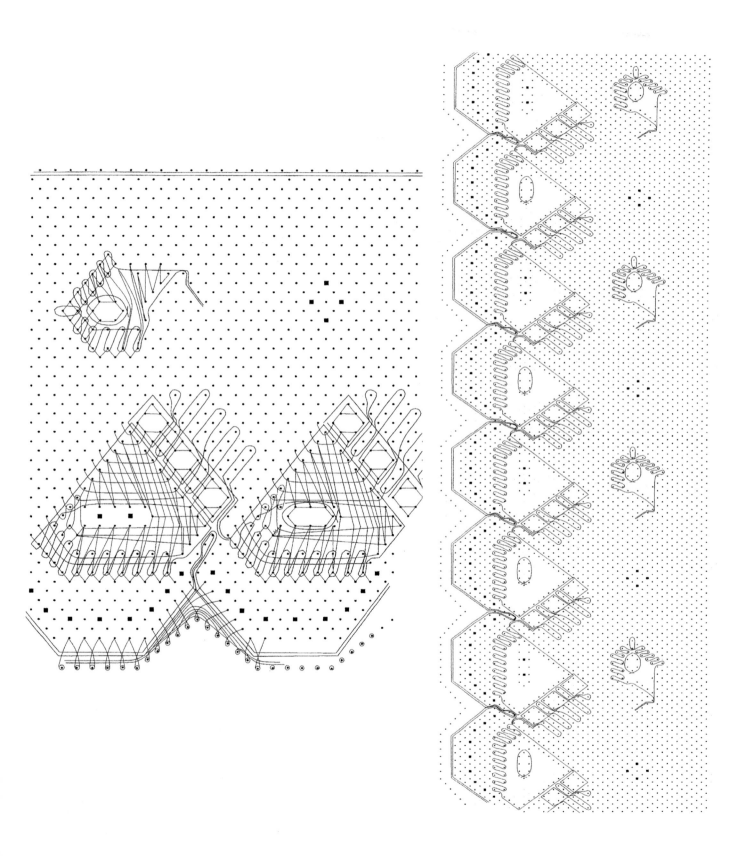

Pattern   PGT97

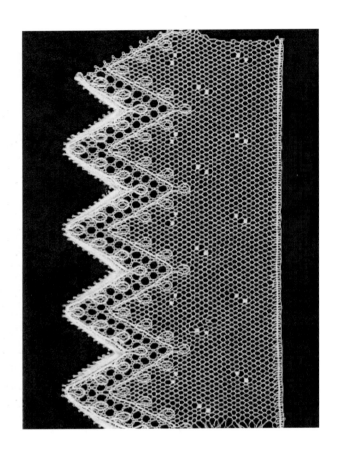

Bobbins	42 pairs
Thread	120/2 Cotton
Gimp	Coton a Broder 30 2 S
Cost per yard	3/8d
1750	£19-28
1830	£9-78

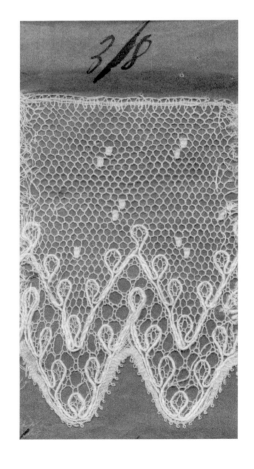

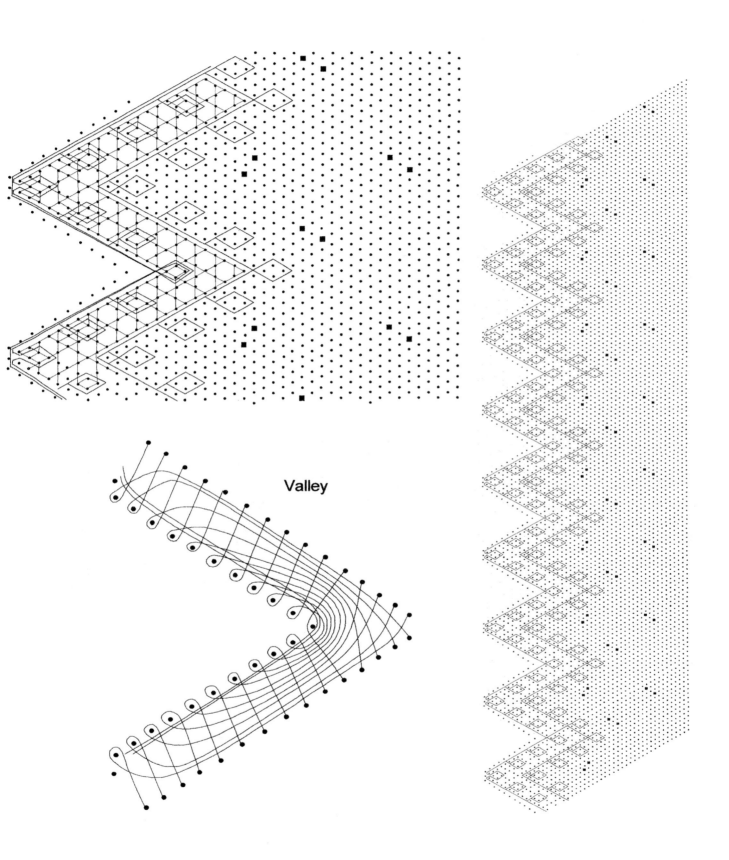

Valley

Pattern   R7

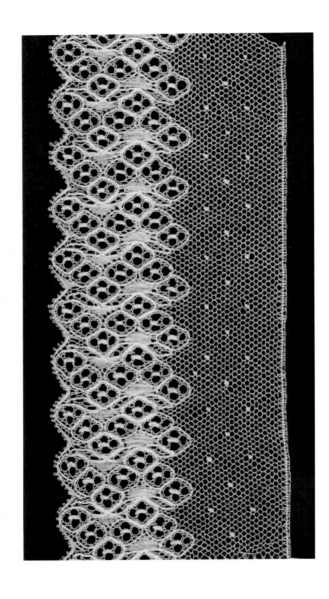

Bobbins	59 pairs
Thread	120/2 Cotton
Gimp	Coton a Broder 25 3 Pr

Cost per yard	3/-
1750	£15-76
1830	£7-98

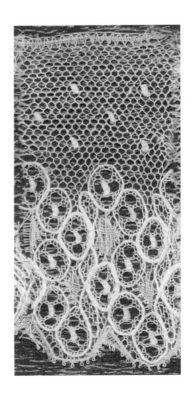

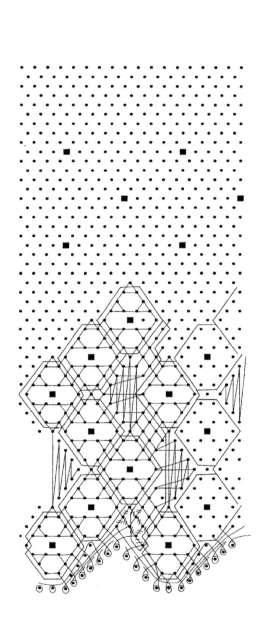

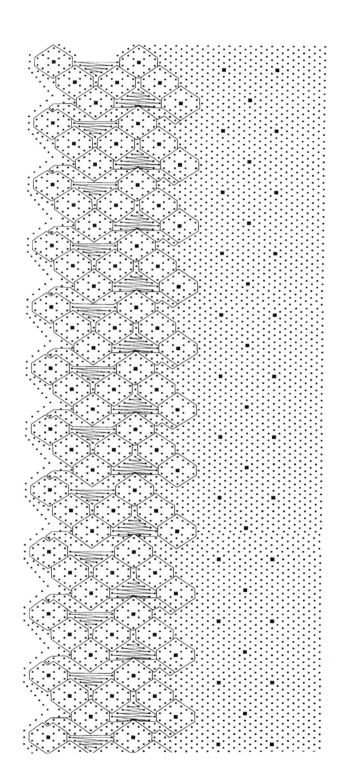

Pattern   PG73

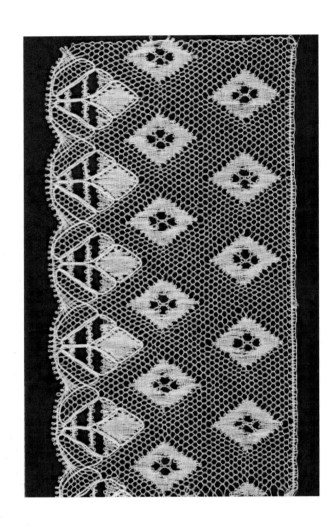

Bobbins	56 pairs
Thread	120/2 Cotton
Gimp	Perle 12 1 Pr
Cost per yard	2/-
1750	£10-50
1830	£-5-40

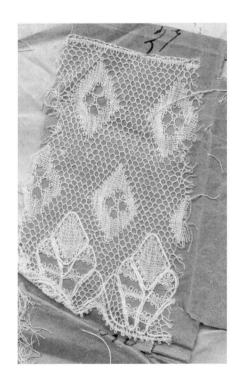